The Demise of the Free State

Dedicated to Professor Kenneth Minogue

A great champion of liberty

Civitas Trustee from 2000-2013

The Demise of the Free State

Why British Democracy and
The EU Don't Mix

David G. Green

Civitas: Institute for the Study of Civil Society
London

First Published March 2014

© Civitas 2014
55 Tufton Street
London SW1P 3QL

email: books@civitas.org.uk

ISBN 978-1-906837-59-4

Independence: Civitas: Institute for the Study of Civil Society is a registered educational charity (No. 1085494) and a company limited by guarantee (No. 04023541). Civitas is financed from a variety of private sources to avoid over-reliance on any single or small group of donors.

All publications are independently refereed. All the Institute's publications seek to further its objective of promoting the advancement of learning. The views expressed are those of the authors, not of the Institute.

Typeset by
Civitas

Printed in Great Britain by
Berforts Group Ltd
Stevenage SG1 2BH

Contents

Author

David G. Green is the Director of Civitas. His books include T*he New Right: The Counter Revolution in Political, Economic and Social Thought*, Wheatsheaf, 1987; *Reinventing Civil Society*, IEA, 1993; *Community Without Politics: A Market Approach to Welfare Reform*, IEA 1996; *Benefit Dependency: How Welfare Undermines Independence*, IEA, 1999; *We're (Nearly) All Victims Now*, Civitas 2006; *Individualists Who Co-operate*, Civitas 2009, *Prosperity with Principles: some policies for economic growth*, Civitas, 2011 and *What Have We Done? The surrender of our democracy to the EU*, Civitas, 2013.

He writes occasionally for newspapers, including in recent years pieces in *The Times* and *The Sunday Times,* the *Sunday Telegraph* and the *Daily Telegraph.*

Preface

This short book has been written because it is tragic to watch my own people, who historically led the way in establishing modern freedom and democracy, absent-mindedly give up our powers of self-government. I have tried to describe what we in the UK have lost in the hope that in the referendum on our EU membership, promised by the Coalition for 2017, we will take back our freedom. Many others have skilfully made the economic case for independence, but it is my conviction that the political and ethical arguments are being neglected. What's at stake is far more than our future prosperity. It's our ability to uphold our distinctive contribution to Western civilisation. The huge cost of the EU is undoubtedly a very important question, but even if the cost were zero – for that matter, even if we made a profit – the case for upholding our independence would stand.

A nation is not just a group of people with a system of government, any more than it is just 'an economy', it is a whole way of living – a civilisation. Along with the peoples of many other countries, we developed what turned out to be the most successful way of life so far discovered: liberal civilisation. Its preservation is the great challenge of our time. Each free people developed its own version of liberal civilisation and ours has been unashamedly individualistic. The freedom sought by individuals was, not merely to be released from con-straints, but the ability to take responsibility for our own lives.

Calling its ethos 'individualistic' risks giving the impression that it was purely self-serving, but on the contrary, liberal civilisation led to a society of individual-ists dedicated to co-operating with others to create charities, mutual societies, commercial enterprises, societies for the advancement of learning, schools, professional associations, and campaigning organisations for all manner of good causes. A vigorous civil society requires a government that leaves space for associations to grow and which creates the legal and institutional structures that sustain them. And it requires a kind of state that welcomes successful, independent associations as a sign of a strong community, not one that is suspicious of private organisations as potential rivals for power. It requires what I will call a 'free state'.

This is the somewhat unfamiliar term I will use for the system of government that is compatible with Britain's liberal civilisation – in which all citizens are able to develop their capabilities to the fullest extent consistent with everyone else enjoying the same freedom.

The style of government favoured by the European Union is very different from the free state that our ancestors fought to develop over many centuries. The single most important element of our constitution is that the government can be thrown out at any time by a simple majority in the House of Commons, and an immediate election called. This possibility remains, but now that fewer of our laws are made by Parliament, the value of being able to hold rulers to account has diminished. The EU makes occasional concessions to democracy here and there, but the primary thrust of the EU project from the outset has been to centralise power in the hands of rulers who have as free a hand as they can get away with. The EU will not change, which means that we need urgently to recover our powers of self-government, while we still have the chance.

David G. Green

Foreword

Controversy about the benefits and disadvantages of UK membership of the European Union commonly focus on practical day-to-day issues. Do we get value for money from our net contribution to EU funds? Do we gain or lose from having about eight per cent of the votes in a large organisation rather than 100 per cent if we were on our own? Is the Social Chapter a plus or a minus? Are we – and particularly the City – drowning under excessive EU regulations or benefiting from being kept safe from dangers to which we would otherwise be exposed? Do we gain or lose from the Single Market?

Matters such as these, important though they are, hide deeper concerns, however, which may go a long way towards explaining why the UK is, on most measures, the most reluctant Member State in the EU. It is not of course just in the UK that the advantages and disadvantages of EU membership are hotly discussed. The debate in the UK, however, tends to have a different feel to it than prevails elsewhere. As David Green very persuasively argues in his pamphlet, much of this stems from the fact that perceptions about the pros and cons of our membership of the EU have a different starting point here than they do on the Continent.

Some of this has to do with history. Because we have not suffered from a successful invasion since 1066, we have been provided with nearly a thousand years during which our nation has gelled together as a unity – much longer than is the case with any other state in Europe. Clearly geography has been important too, providing the UK with far more clearly defined boundaries than those which have been constantly moved and changed on the continent. More significant than either of these influences, however, may be the way in which political organisation has developed over a long period in the UK compared with what happened on the other side of the channel. Whereas until comparatively recently nearly all of continental Europe experienced long periods of top-down authoritarian government, in the UK it has been different. For centuries, authority has ultimately stemmed from the people and not the ruler. The state has been there to serve the citizen and not the other way round.

Even before 1066, English kings were far from absolute monarchs. Although, in most other areas over which they held sway, the Normans tended strongly to authoritarian rule, in England their regime gradually adapted to the more consensual arrangements which have always prevailed on our side of the channel. The terms set out in Magna Carta were conceded in 1215. By the early Middle Ages, Parliament was beginning to find its feet. The judiciary gradually achieved a degree of independence for which there was little equivalence almost anywhere else. Inevitably, there were ebbs and flows. The Tudors and Stuarts tried hard, with varying degrees of success, to establish the right of monarchs to rule as they saw fit. Crucially, they failed to do so, leading to the expulsion of James II and the Glorious Revolution.

The last three centuries then saw the slow emergence of full representative democracy, based on the tolerance and communal spirit which made it possible. It is no co-incidence that the Industrial Revolution, which transformed humanity's prospects, started in the free and stable conditions that prevailed in the UK. It was also the economic power which industrialisation made possible that enabled British people to establish by far the largest empire the world has ever seen. Perhaps its most important consequence has been to create the

Anglosphere, all of which shares the rule of law, Habeas Corpus, trial by jury, enforceable contracts, freedom of speech and the press, crowned by parliaments or their equivalents, whose members are elected in free and fair elections, holding the executive to account.

The crucial issue raised in David Green's pamphlet is whether this approach to the way in which the state should be organised and the relationship it should have with its citizens is compatible with the way in which the EU operates. With ample evidence, he shows how great the difficulties are and why this is so important and significant for the way events may evolve in future.

The UK joined what was then the Common Market in 1973 at a time when our imperial role was rapidly disappearing and our economy was in deep disarray. It was our lack of self-confidence in 1975 which persuaded two thirds of those who voted in the only referendum ever held on our membership that there was no future for us unless we stayed in. History since then, however, has shown that the instinct of those who opposed continuing membership, based at least partly on concern that we were foregoing the priceless advantages of our democratic system of government, had much more to be said for it than might have appeared to be the case at the time. It is not a coincidence that the economic success enjoyed by the original Six has melted away as top down economic policies – the Snake, the Exchange Rate Mechanism and now the Single Currency, all the antithesis of Anglo-Saxon pragmatism – caused the growth rate in what is now the EU to plummet, and support for it to wither.

Most of this occurred because there is no effective democracy in the EU of the type developed over the centuries in the UK, which might have stopped these mistakes being made. The EU crucially lacks democratic accountability and hence the electoral support and endorsement it so badly needs. As this pamphlet scathingly says, to much too great an extent, there is no European demos, no shared culture, no confidence that groups will not seek to take advantage, no sense of the common good, no shared story of how we got to where we are today, no common view of obligations to future generations, no shared approach to law, and no common attitude to personal freedom, individual responsibility, civil society and the pursuit of public purposes in organised private life. Instead there is a classic case of producer capture with unelected officials having too much power to run the EU in ways which suit themselves rather than those who would like to be able to elect and to dismiss them.

It is hardly surprising, in these circumstances, that it is the UK which is taking the lead in pressing for radical reform in the EU and a return to free trade rather than the 'ever closer union' beloved of the EU's founders, who had much more faith in officials than politicians. It is not difficult to see why, half-way through the twentieth century, this was a widely shared view among many continental leaders. A thousand years of history have taught the British something different, however, and this is why more and more people in the UK are coming to agree with David Green's thesis that democracy and the EU don't mix.

John Mills

Introduction

Europe has a torn political history on two dimensions: on the one hand between freedom and uniformity; and on the other between constitutional democracy and authoritarianism. Some regimes have set out to impose one prescribed 'correct' way of life and others have championed the personal freedom to discover the right way to live. And some have favoured absolutist rulers while others have preferred democratic accountability. In this great struggle the British people have always been on the side of freedom and liberal-democracy, while the EU inclines towards uniformity and unaccountable elite rule.

Some enthusiasts for the EU may resist the conclusion that their ambitions will undermine freedom and democracy. They have convinced themselves that they represent the best in European achievement. We must ask them to question their own beliefs and to ask why liberal civilisation has thrived in Europe. My argument is that the free state is the key accomplishment: government that is both accountable to its people and dedicated to their personal freedom. The EU is not altogether lacking in democratic institutions, but its structure is calculated to concentrate power in a few hands. Nor is it completely without tolerance for national differences, but its appetite for imposing harmonisation puts it well along the road that leads from liberty to uniformity. In almost every respect it is leading us away from the ideals and the institutions that have been fundamental to liberal civilisation.

Members of the European Commission, which comprises the heads of the EU's permanent bureaucracy, try to portray the champions of exit as self-serving, and to paint themselves as supporters of international co-

1

operation who renounce narrow nationalism. But, when we in Britain fight to preserve our own heritage of freedom and democracy, we are not merely defending our own interests. By resisting the encroachments of the Brussels bureaucracy, we are also fighting for the freedom of other peoples and defending the most precious traditions of European civilisation. We have many potential allies throughout Europe and we should make common cause with them wherever possible.

Nor are we engaged only in a struggle about how best to organise domestic political systems. We also represent the tradition of international co-operation that is founded on respect for the independence of other peoples – an approach that seeks out mutual benefits and avoids the imposition of a solitary view. The EU bureaucracy tries to portray its opponents as narrow nationalists who are hostile to international co-operation. But the real dispute is about the best form of international relations: on the one hand, the association of mutually respectful liberal democracies accountable to their own peoples, or on the other, subordination to a would-be super state that aims to exert external force. The Brussels vision is not even truly international – it's more about constructing a regional power bloc than finding a worldwide structure that will encourage peace rather than war, promote the mutual benefits of trade, and increase the free exchange of knowledge and understanding. I will argue, not only that independent nation states are vital for the protection of liberty, democracy and opportunity, but also that independent nations are the most mutually beneficial basis for international relations. Britain, of course, has joined many international bodies – including the UN, NATO, the Commonwealth, the IMF, the WTO, and the World Bank. In many cases, they involve compromises with other countries, but the difference is that the EU is a replacement for the nation state, rather than a limited inter-state agreement.

It is bewildering that a country like ours with such a proud history of upholding freedom and democracy has allowed its capacity for self-government to drain away to Brussels. One cause has been the failure of our schools to teach an objective account of our own history, leaving our young people bereft of understanding of the strengths and weaknesses of our system. It is vital, therefore, to remind ourselves of the precious political and cultural heritage left by earlier generations who fought to make possible a free and democratic life for all citizens of this land.

The argument is organised as follows. Chapter 1 summarises the main elements of liberal civilisation and especially the distinctive idea of individualism as moral, practical and intellectual independence. This is the heritage being put at risk by our EU membership. Chapter 2 is a shortened version of a previously-published pamphlet, *What Have We Done? The surrender of our democracy to the EU,* which describes how our system of government developed from Anglo-Saxon times. Rather than putting readers to the trouble of digging out the earlier text, I thought it would be more convenient to include the descriptive sections (with some updating and a reply to critics of the earlier version) in the current publication. Chapter 3 tries to understand how we lost our way, and Chapter 4 touches briefly on the importance of the independent nation state for maintaining a liberal international order.

1

Liberal Civilisation and the Free State

The political achievement of which we can be most proud is the development of the 'free state', a system of government committed to creating conditions that encourage the full development of all the beneficial capabilities of every citizen. This accomplishment is now threatened by our continued membership of an expansionist EU. Calling a nation state devoted to personal freedom a 'free state' distinguishes it from theories that look upon freedom as the absence of state action. In this latter view, every reduction in the powers of government is a gain for freedom. The free state, however, rests on the assumption that freedom depends on active government – going further than protecting individuals from crime and ensuring that no one is without the basic necessities required to be able to develop their capacities to the full. It also marks it out from theories that favour extensions of state power going beyond what is necessary to safeguard personal freedom. The free state is not the minimal state and it is not the omnipotent state. It is the name for a political theory that puts the individual in society at the heart of things. That is to say, it is a system of limited government that is not hostile to government as such, but rather recognises the importance of skilful government in discharging the primary task of the state – upholding personal freedom. To speak favourably about skilful government may seem like heresy to some defenders of a free society, but there is a long tradition of recognising the importance of active government for upholding freedom.

Henry Simons, one of the outstanding generation of economists and philosophers at the University of Chicago who steadfastly defended freedom just before and after the Second World War, famously wrote about 'A positive program for laissez faire'.[1] Writing during the Great Depression of the 1930s, Simons strongly argued that government had not fulfilled one of its primary duties when it failed to regulate the banks and control the money supply. Few things, he thought, more readily destroyed individual freedom than runaway inflation. Friedrich Hayek (also at the University of Chicago from 1950 until 1962) argued that: 'There is ... all the difference between deliberately creating a system within which competition will work as beneficially as possible, and passively accepting institutions as they are.' Nothing has done as much harm, he thought, as 'the wooden insistence of some liberals' on *laissez faire*.[2] The important challenge was to accomplish the 'gradual improvement of the institutional framework of a free society', a task that implies active government. Government can get too big for its boots, but the size of government should not be the sole concern of liberals. The primary aim should be to keep government focused on upholding freedom. A government that stands to one side as a matter of habit may leave power in the hands of powerful private organisations that pursue their own interests at the general expense and narrow the freedom of the majority.

The free state and its civic culture

It is difficult to surpass John Stuart Mill's explanation of why representative democracy matters. A democratic system assumes that it will be advantageous if all citizens can influence the decisions of their government. It takes it for granted that they are in command of moral and intellectual qualities that could improve the actions of the state.[3]

As a result, Mill argued that there were two measures of the merit of any government. The most important was how much it promoted the virtues of its people – in Mill's language, the moral, intellectual and active qualities of its citizens. The second was how far its machinery took advantage of the good qualities that existed at any one time. A representative constitution was a way of bringing the general standard of intelligence and virtue to bear on government. The greater the extent to which good qualities could have an impact, the better the system for everyone. The ideal was an electorate high in intellectual, moral and active capabilities that was allowed to exert a strong influence on government. But we can imagine nations with a well-informed public whose members are prevented by political institutions from influencing leaders; and we can envisage political institutions open to influence by the electorate but disadvantaged by a public too ill-informed, passive, or inattentive to play a part.

In the light of Mill's criteria, how well does EU governance compare with Britain's political heritage? What has been the contribution of the European Union to the great struggle between democracy and personal freedom on the one hand, and unaccountable government and uniformity on the other? The true intentions of the elite that dominates the EU were openly stated by President Barroso in his 2012 'state of the union' address.

He revealed the hostile attitude of the Commission to member states. In its efforts to create a political union, the EU had to choose between the 'soft power' of 'political persuasion' and what he called the 'nuclear option' of Article 7 (which allows for the suspension of the rights of member states). There was a need for a public prosecutor to uphold the 'rule of law', by which he meant to impose obedience to the will of the Commission. He thought national democracies led to 'fragmentation' and said that leaders must learn to follow the lead of the Commission to political union and avoid 'national provincialism'. The EU 'must not allow the populists and the nationalists to set up a negative agenda'. The term 'populism' is Brussels code for democracy and 'nationalism' is disagreeing with the Brussels elite. Other leaders of the campaign to extend EU power at the expense of nation states have often made no secret of their contempt for democracy. Claude Cheysson, French foreign minister under President Mitterrand, boasted in 1999 that the Maastricht Treaty, which transferred vast powers from member states to the EU, was only possible because democratic methods had been side-stepped: 'The construction of Europe has taken place because of inter-governmental cooperation. We worked outside the normal democratic structures and that is why we succeeded.'[4]

If the pronouncements of the President in his 2012 speech are a fair indication of the intentions of Europe's rulers, then the EU does not picture itself as the next stage in the evolution of liberty and democracy. It is a grand power-building project that has set itself up in rivalry to the main institution that has protected Europe's traditions of freedom and self-government: the free state based on democratic legitimacy at home and respect for the freedom of other nations. The EU is a system dominated by officials who seek to set up a European identity to rival that of its member states, while carefully tending to their own interests. As Lee Rotherham has shown, EU officials are amply remunerated and enjoy perks available to few ordinary employees.[5]

There is an intellectual tradition of treating national loyalty as a primitive emotion to be overcome. Einstein saw nationality as a kind of disease: 'the measles of the human race'.[6] H.G. Wells thought we were citizens of the world and he hoped for the final achievement of world-wide political and social unity. Our true nationality was mankind.[7] The EU's ruling elite has a tendency to go even further and treat all nationalisms as if they resemble the German variety of the 1930s and 1940s. But Nazism was a perversion of nationality that used national symbols to dragoon citizens into supporting military action against foreigners as well as to incite aggression against minorities within Germany. Western civilisation was saved by a very different kind of national feeling: the self-sacrificing patriotism of the British, Americans, the free French, New Zealanders, Australians, Canadians, Indians and other allies. Their spirit of national allegiance encouraged people to risk their own lives for the freedom of others. German nationalism was aggressive. Nevertheless, EU leaders regularly condemn all nationalism rather than Germany's perversion of it.

In recent years the value of the nation state has been re-appraised by writers across the political spectrum. Roger Scruton, Kenneth Minogue and Charles Moore have re-examined it from a liberal-conservative vantage point and David Miller and David Goodhart have looked at it from the perspective of those who want to use the power of the state to create equal opportunities.[8] Moreover, some economists are at long last recognising that their narrow utilitarian calculus misses out much that explains why some nations are prosperous and others are not.[9] And now the Labour party has chosen to

8

differentiate itself from 'old Labour' and 'new Labour' by using the term 'one-nation Labour'. Under the leadership of Maurice Glasman, Jon Cruddas, Jonathan Rutherford, Marc Stears and others, the nation state is well on the way to rehabilitation as a legitimate political idea. I will focus on Britain's sense of nationality, but much of the argument applies to other countries too. (Some say that we should speak of the component parts of the UK, but we have a long tradition of concentric allegiances: we can be English and British, as well as Welsh, Scottish or Irish and British.)

It has often been remarked that we can understand ourselves better by paying attention to what outsiders say about us. A German scholar, Wilhelm Dibelius, wrote about England after the First World War to try to understand the nature of the people who had defeated Germany. He offers a useful starting point. English civilisation, he thought, had been an achievement of the rank and file and their culture, not their leaders.[10] England, he concluded, could live without great individuals for comparatively longer than any other country:

> ... men, simple, of average endowment, and little or no intellectual or artistic claims, who quite naturally, good-naturedly, and egotistically pushed with their elbows and kept on making the world more and more English: men who, at any crisis were slow to sacrifice themselves, but when there was nothing else for it, came forward and did what was necessary.[11]

He detected a willingness to accept leadership, but only so long as it sought to inspire and not to compel. Self-control, he thought, was the instinct of the nation. Children were taught to expect nothing, except from their own exertions. But this attitude had not made for a purely self-centred people. Free play was given to initiatives that built social institutions. This spirit, he said, freed slaves, expanded charity, developed mutual aid, evolved manufacturing, and nourished scientists and engineers.[12]

Is there truth in his interpretation? How should we understand Britain at its best? Even if we have not always lived up to our own ideals, this is the heritage we stand to lose if we continue to allow the EU to erode our ability to govern ourselves.

What do we believe in? What holds us together? Like many other nation states our allegiance is territorial. We have a territory or homeland, which defines where the state's jurisdiction applies and we have an allegiance to common beliefs which are intimately bound up with this homeland. It is a form of solidarity that is not tribal, ethnic or religious, but based on shared values. Anyone can become a British citizen, so long as they live here and are committed to our way of life. German nationalism under Hitler, by contrast, was not territorial but racial.

One of the most fundamental beliefs is that we have a collective past and a future. This feeling of historical continuity is captured by a national story of achievement – in our own case the struggle to build freedom and democracy described in Chapter 2. To be British is to belong to an active community that puts duties on the living generations to uphold something precious for those who are to follow, and not merely to think of their own interests. When we act together we have an active moral identity, and may speak of shame or pride about past events. Take slavery. Should we be proud that we helped to end it? Or should we be ashamed to have been involved in the first place; or both?[13]

In common with other nations, we also have a public or civic culture. We see ourselves as a free people and take pride in our democracy because it prevents the abuse of power by ensuring popular consent and making possible the peaceful removal of governments.[14] The mainstream civic culture is liberal – it is about upholding a free state that makes rules so that individuals can co-operate. But the civic culture is not monolithic and allows space for rival views about the common good. There is machinery for finding a mutual accommodation, or a *modus vivendi*. It calls upon every group to avoid using state coercion selfishly. It is a framework for bringing out the best in people, which depends on trust born of reciprocity.

In some territories these commitments are absent and in such cases it may be better for a state to divide. In 1993, for example, Czechoslovakia found that the solidarity and trust necessary for self-government were not present. It divided peacefully into two nations: the Czech Republic and Slovakia. This successful separation highlights a vital feature of the nation-state. It is the workable unit for 'give and take'. The rights entailed by membership of a nation are claims against others and can be used selfishly. In recent years, for example, 'human rights' have frequently become one-sided demands – most infamously when foreign criminals seeking to avoid deportation have sired children, in whom they take little practical interest, and then used them to claim a human right to 'family life'. But rights and duties are only feasible in a nation state where there is widespread trust that power will not be abused either by individuals or by political opponents. Rights need to be protected from people who would bend and manipulate them to self-serving ends. In Britain we accept that power can change hands because there is enough trust between us to allow the opposing party to take office. When this basic loyalty is eroded, self-restraint tends to diminish. A civic culture that promotes the common good cannot be taken for granted. As Fukuyama has shown, political cultures differ considerably. In some cases, local representatives do not go to their political capitals to seek the public good, but to bring back to their locality a share of the spoils.[15]

Our famously unwritten constitution confines government to its proper tasks, but also allows it to act on behalf of the whole people. The state can act for everyone and be held to account. If its responsibilities are kept to a manageable size, then policies can be treated as experiments whose success or failure can be judged by citizens. Over the years, there have been sharp differences about the proper scope of the state and its role has changed radically in the last few decades. The welfare state, for example, has been constantly reformed and now benefit recipients are required to take a job when only a few years ago such conditions were seen as unduly harsh. An accountable government can soon be put under pressure to correct its mistakes and to reflect prevailing opinion.

Our system is one of liberty under law, with the law protecting personal initiative but always within a culture that encourages a strong allegiance to other members of society. We are a nation of individualists who co-operate.[16] Law-making long ago ceased to be the issuing of commands by a personal ruler. It became the act of a sovereign people who gave their consent to laws through representative institutions. The phrase 'the rule of law' came to mean a 'government of laws' made with the consent of the people, as opposed to government based on the personal proclamations of the ruler (discussed further in Chapter 2). Some discretion exercised by officials was unavoidable, but as Chapter 2 will show,

Parliament fought to ensure that such power was granted only to office holders who could be removed by Parliament.

Moreover, any law would not do. Laws were only seen as legitimate if they sought to protect freedom. By limiting the scope of the state, the law left space for personal judgement. Because the main perceived risk was that factions would abuse law-making power, laws were required, not only to be subject to consent by the governed, but also to serve the common good and to apply equally to all.[17] There were to be no laws for specific classes (such as the clergy) and laws must be impartially enforced. Judges continue to swear this oath: 'I will do right by all manner of people, after the law and usages of this realm, without fear or favour, affection or ill will.'

Liberal civilisation: individualism and a moral life

So far I have focused on our political institutions and culture, but earlier I claimed that we had contributed to the emergence of liberal civilisation. How should we understand its main elements?

Above all, it is a civilisation based on the practice of freedom. We often call ourselves a capitalist society and so when we speak of freedom we think first of commercial freedom of action. But leading a free life means far more, and touches every area of human existence including religion, science, music, the visual arts, warfare, and our personal moral struggles to be good family members, friends, neighbours and work colleagues. In the earliest days of emerging liberalism, the desire for freedom of worship was far more important than the wish for commercial freedom.[18]

Our political system evolved over several centuries to ensure government by consent, and in particular to prevent absolutism, but liberal civilisation can't be fully understood without recognising that it was also a struggle for a new kind of moral order. Historically, the struggle in Britain and in many other countries was against a social order based on obedience and submission, perhaps governed by a sacred text or a personal ruler with absolute power. Such societies were gradually replaced by those based on knowledge acquired through public discussion and trial and error. In the early days of what was later called liberalism, notably in the writings of Milton, the aim of reformers was freedom of conscience: free examination of religious beliefs rather than coercion by authority. Milton famously asked in *Areopagitica*, 'Who ever knew Truth put to the worse, in a free and open encounter?'[19] Milton particularly defended freedom of discussion as a safeguard against error. Religious authorities should not dictate doctrine because to do so could mean forcing people to accept factual mistakes as true propositions. Moreover, a coerced act of worship had no moral merit.

Why did the pioneers of liberal civilisation think accountable government, open to public criticism, would be better than absolutism? Their underlying assumption was human fallibility. No one, including rulers, knows everything and open government helps to prevent bad rulers from doing too much harm. We all progress towards a better understanding with the aid of others. It may emerge from a rough and ready public debate or from a highly organised process, as in science. As Mill pointed out (above), the aim was individual moral and intellectual growth. Ultimately, absolutism was disliked because it failed to develop capacities and, therefore, wasted talent.

As Professor Kenneth Minogue skilfully explains, we can't understand liberal civilisation unless we understand its distinctive view of the individual. A life of freedom entails leading a moral life of discovering right and wrong, and of working out the best course of action. Minogue captures the essential liberal idea by contrasting servility with individualism. Individualism should not be confused with egoism, which could mean following inner drives without reflection, a kind of 'slavishness' that is considered a moral failure. The freedom celebrated by liberals incorporated limitation; whereas the goal of liberation does not.[20] Liberalism was not sheer wilfulness, an observation that arises constantly in liberal writing. Locke had contrasted liberty and licence[21] and early eighteenth-century defenders of freedom spoke of 'virtuous liberty'.[22] According to Joseph Addison, founder of the *Spectator*, writing in the play *Cato:* 'A day, an hour, of virtuous liberty / Is worth a whole eternity in bondage'. Kant distinguished between wild freedom and civil freedom, and Edmund Burke famously argued that people with 'intemperate minds' cannot be free. Their passions 'forge their fetters':

> Men are qualified for civil liberty in exact proportion to their disposition to put moral chains upon their own appetites ... in proportion as they are more disposed to listen to the counsels of the wise and good, in preference to the flattery of knaves. Society cannot exist, unless a controlling power upon will and appetite be placed somewhere; and the less of it there is within, the more there must be without.[23]

These writers recognised that the individualism that lay at the core of liberal civilisation can sound like a surrender to impulse, and fully recognised that civilisation depends on the control of impulses.[24] For them, the real dispute was about who was in control of

15

impulses. In customary or authoritarian societies, doing the right thing meant being obedient to authority. Anything else was doing the wrong thing. Individualism was therefore seen as non-conformity. Liberal individualism emphasised *self-imposed* limits. Liberals did not like anyone telling them to conform, but they accepted that a functioning society depended on self-control. Many religions have tried to encourage a genuine commitment to their faith rather than mere outward compliance, thus implying a moral struggle, facing up to doubt, and leading a coherent moral life based on commitments each individual has personally made.

Many feared that, without self-imposed constraints on violent or self-serving impulses, the development of a free society would be endangered. Throughout Europe, writers were conscious of the massive slaughter of the 30 Years War – thought to be greater as a proportion of the population than in any other war. It ended in 1648, but Europeans continued for many generations to encounter the fury that could easily be provoked by religious as well as other differences. In the seventeenth century England had gone through a long civil war, which made the great majority determined to avoid the destructive effects of violence and hatred. The aim was to enact constitutional rules that increased the chances that policies would be made following calm and measured discussion and to prevent temporary majorities forcing decisions through in a rush. Different religions had each experienced persecution. Royalists had used the power of the state against their opponents, and then paid heavily in the age of Cromwell, only to take their revenge after the Restoration of 1660. The result was that by the time of the Revolution of 1688-89, all the powerful groups came to see the value of denying absolute power to all sectional interests, including themselves.[25] Acton, in his great essay on the history of freedom, put it like this:

> sanctifying freedom and consecrating it to God, teaching men to treasure the liberties of others as their own, and to defend them for love of justice and charity more than as a claim of right, has been the soul of what is great and good in the progress of the last two hundred years.[26]

The same fears guided the founders of the American republic when they framed their constitution in the 1780s.[27] In their anxiety to slow down the power of majorities, they created a potential for deadlock that has led to eighteen partial government shutdowns, including one in 2013.

The intellectual roots of liberal civilisation can be discerned in Greek times when Socrates stood out against the community at the cost of his own life. The moral of the story was that individuals could be right and majorities wrong. Minogue disagrees with Isaiah Berlin that freedom is best seen as a purely 'negative' idea. He is not saying that 'positive' freedom is better than 'negative' freedom. He would have shared Hayek's view that the absence of coercion ('negative' freedom) is valuable in itself, just as peace (the absence of war) is valuable on its own. And he would have agreed that power, which is often what is meant by 'positive' freedom, should not be confused with being free from constraints that suppress the ability to plan and choose the course of your life. Minogue's point is that, in practice, liberals valued freedom because it encouraged a particular type of character – the kind of independent people for whom a handshake was binding. In other words, freedom was inextricably bound up with virtues of a certain kind. Sincere liberals preferred honest, independent, brave people who participated in political and civic life, volunteered to help strangers, met their own family obligations, and saw work as a vocation. And they looked upon democracy, not as the exertion of power over others, but as government by people who were capable of self-government.[28]

The obvious concern was that, if there was to be individual choice of moral code, what was to prevent society disintegrating into a mass of squabbling individuals or factions certain of their own righteousness? That is why intellectually consistent liberals emphasise self-criticism more than self-assertion. Critical reason should always start with self-criticism and lead from there to mutual criticism.[29] It is not pure iconoclasm.

There is no doubt that much of the language of early liberalism is about release from custom but it only made sense within societies already used to living under law. For Minogue, individualism and law are 'inseparable partners'.[30] And as we have seen, liberal individualism was also liberation into a moral context that was demanding. But this moral climate was very different from the custom that stipulated a complete way of life.

Individualism in Europe began as a revolt against political authority and religious orthodoxy. The Whigs were particularly hostile to 'priestcraft'. A prime example they had in mind was the decision of the Church to force Galileo to recant his findings about the relative movement of the Sun and the Earth, a story of reason struggling against imposed orthodoxy. Often, however, religious dissenters were people who simply wanted to worship in a distinctive way, such as Quakers, whose practices had little connection with either reason or science. Nevertheless, Christian ideas paved the way for the emergence of liberal individualism, specifically the idea of people as creatures of passions that religion sought to contain. Christianity accepted the idea of an inner struggle between a higher self and a lower self. This struggle involved a release from enforced conformity, not to 'anything goes' but to freely-accepted self-discipline. The ideal of Christianity at its best was a moral life seen as a continuous process of self-understanding: we respond to external influences and to our own inner life. The struggle was no longer between the 'powers that be' and the individual but within the mind of each person, engaging at once with others around them but also with their own conscience. Liberal individualism was not 'isolated' individualism. Individual self-management inevitably demanded that the moral agents should cultivate human relationships, including a life of association in clubs, charities and churches.[31] For this reason, many churches had a strong communal life, especially the independent congregations that chose their own leaders and came to play a central role in the political struggles of the seventeenth century.

Much confusion has been caused by versions of socialism that originated in opposition to individualism and insisted that the individual was not a 'social atom'. But 'atomised individualism' was not the guiding light of liberal civilisation. The claim that man was a 'social being' was not denied. We have many relations within society. Indeed, we can only acquire self-respect in association with other people. To speak of individualism does not imply an atomised society. It is strongly associated with obligations to family and commitment to one's vocation.[32]

Today's champions of freedom tend not to focus on the freedom to lead a moral life. They are more likely to be thinking of freedom of action in commerce, or complete release from moral constraints, especially any obligations to children resulting from casual sexual liaisons. Personal freedom made possible the unrivalled prosperity of the West, but prosperity was never the primary focus, and we can't understand commercial freedom unless we understand the moral freedom that preceded it. Individuals were assumed to have an inner moral life that was forever developing, and they were expected to be armed with powers of fortitude and self-control. Individuals have often been called autonomous, but typically this meant able to exercise judgement within the agreed rules. It was not the autonomy of ignoring everyone else; but rather the autonomy of self-criticism and acquiring the ability to make independent criticisms of prevailing views. Intellectually consistent liberal sceptics are most critical of themselves.

According to one of the foremost interpreters of liberalism, Guido Ruggiero, liberal civilisation demanded much of the individual:

> Freedom deprives a man of the comfortable support of ready-made decisions from without, which save him the pains of inner struggle; it leaves him naked in the sight of his conscience, burdened with the unshared responsibility for his own actions, which no kindly authority can conceal or disguise.[33]

The ultimate spirit of liberal civilisation has found expression when individuals have been tested to the limits of endurance. Writing about his time in the Auschwitz concentration camp, Viktor Frankl said that even in the face of the most evil cruelty he realised that there was one thing the Nazis could not take from him: his own attitude to what they were doing to him. 'In a position of utter desolation,' he wrote, the only achievement available to an individual 'may consist in enduring his sufferings in the right way—an honourable way.'[34]

We can gain some further insight into the liberal idea of a free moral life by contrasting it with the modern idea of 'political correctness'. Liberal civilisation implied a rejection of systems that expected nothing but individual obedience enforced by punishments. It also implied a rejection of 'slavishness' of two kinds. First, submitting to mere impulses, such as hatred, did not require judgement; and, second, subservience to prevailing opinion was seen as a similar kind of conformism, involving no conscious judgement. Sociologist Norman Dennis has convincingly argued that many modern social-policy intellectuals are mere conformists who slavishly follow habits of thought without understanding. During the 1970s and 1980s it became common for members of the social-policy intelligentsia to take for granted the idea that all lifestyles are equally valid and to contend that we must never judge other cultures. It was also common to denounce prevailing factual beliefs as nothing more than reflections of the interests of a ruling elite who manipulated the social order to their own advantage. Postmodernists, along with old-fashioned Marxists, condemned liberal civilisation as culturally specific. The idea of a mutual search for objective truth was rejected. Mutual self-criticism was not seen as relevant. For writers such as Marcuse, Horkheimer and Adorno, 'facticity' or the 'factual mentality' were bourgeois devices for exercising control.[35] There was no such thing as objective truth, only Western values. Nietzsche was the favourite analyst of many: 'There are no truths, only interpretations', he had once claimed.[36]

Their ideas amount to a rejection of the very possibility of pursuing truth and understanding through public discussion and social experiment, and Dennis contends that many social scientists in the 1980s who subscribed to this doctrine had no idea of its earlier association with Marxism or revisionist Marxism that rejected liberal civilisation. They entertained their ideas with the same kind of lazy ritual observance found in some religions. In a university, however, such conformism is an abandonment of the central purpose of the institution.

This stock of ideas came to be called 'political correctness', a term that implies obedience to previously laid down stipulations. Politically correct (PC) thinking is imitative rather than deliberative.[37] Members of the social-policy intelligentsia who think they are being avant-garde are in reality intellectual conformists following the prevailing orthodoxies like sheep. We may hope that the gut hostility felt by many people to modern PC thinking suggests that the older liberal idea of individual moral struggle is still instinctively understood. If not, we have started to turn our backs on the Enlightenment project.

To summarise the argument so far: liberal individualism was never seen as mere wilfulness. It was freedom under law. Moreover, individuals were not perceived as bearers of mere wants or desires, but as guided by conscience. It was the kind of freedom that put the burden of decision on the individual. It was not just about throwing off constraints, but transferring responsibilities to individuals organised in civil society.

The empire builders in Brussels have little or no respect for Europe's liberal civilisation. They belong to the collectivist tradition of European thought that mistrusted liberal-democracy and saw the leaders of the state as the best judges of the real interests of the people. They are not full-blooded authoritarians, nor are they exactly like the monarchs of old, but they seek to centralise power in their own hands. By doing so, they reduce the scope for the exercise of individual conscience and for the advancement of civilisation through the co-operative endeavours of free citizens. Within a liberal civilisation the task of the state is to create the space for moral agency and free co-operation. The Brussels bureaucracy continuously narrows the realm of conscience and widens the realm of coercion.

Individualism in practice

What were the practical results of liberal individualism? The freedom under law that emerged in Britain after the Revolution of 1688 did not imply a retreat into the pleasures of private life. Many public purposes were now seen as a private responsibility. Freedom demanded much of the individual, and this transfer of obligations was taken seriously. Freedom for everyone entailed the assumption that individuals should not suffer privations that prevented them from keeping body and mind together. Citizens could always fall back on the bare minimum provided by the Poor Law, but a range of institutions tried to protect people from having to resort to it, and there were countless charities for every conceivable need. In the eighteenth century charities were founded for the relief of poverty, to combat disease, to spread learning, to assist the infirm or elderly, to provide libraries, to rescue abandoned children, to overcome the exploitation of children, and much more.[38]

Charity was so widely available that, at one of the high points of laissez faire in the mid-nineteenth century, a common complaint was that there was too much charity and that it was constantly abused. The Charity Organisation Society famously campaigned against 'unthinking' charities. In *Charity and Social Life*, C.S. Loch argued that some endowed charities had tended to create a 'permanent demand' for relief, much like modern welfare dependency. Such charities 'often foster pauperism instead of preventing it'.[39] Henry Mayhew, who is famous for highlighting the state of London's poor in the 1850s and 1860s, also described how the good intentions of many donors were exploited. The begging-letter writer was, he said, foremost among beggars.[40] To this day, the term 'begging letter' has pejorative connotations.

More important than charities, measured by the number of people for whom provision was made, were organisations for mutual aid. Relying on charity was often considered to be a personal failing and, as a result, many people set up mutual aid associations. For those unable to earn enough to guarantee their own independence, mutual aid societies developed to guarantee it as a group member.[41] Everyone paid small weekly or regular amounts into a common fund on which members could draw in adversity. By 1910, just before national insurance was introduced, there were 6.6m registered members of friendly societies, a number greater than the combined membership of the trade unions and co-operative societies. (There were 2.5m members of registered trade unions and 2.5m members of co-operative societies.)[42]

Some later critics found these arrangements wanting and called for a welfare state, but that debate is for another day. The issue at present is not to discover whether this multitude of private arrangements was better or worse than provision by government agencies, it is merely to point out that, when given the freedom to control their own affairs, the result was not the chaos anticipated by authoritarians, but rather that countless individuals put their efforts into developing some of the finest institutions known to human history.

In the eighteenth century, support also grew rapidly for religions of conscience, such as Methodism, rather than faiths satisfied by minimal outward observance, such as the Church of England.[43] And what we now call 'public opinion' began to emerge. Public campaigns for political outcomes developed, most famously the campaign against slavery, which brought the slave trade to an end by 1807, and slavery in the British Empire to an end by 1833, despite the huge economic costs.[44]

The centrality of the ideal of a moral life also explains the growing readership of novels in the era of individualism, especially those about moral conflict.[45] Many books of that time continue to be valued today. Bunyan's *Pilgrim's Progress* was published in 1678 and was widely read over the next 200 years, some say nearly as widely read as the Bible. Daniel Defoe's *Robinson Crusoe* came out in 1719, Jonathan Swift's *Gulliver's Travels* in 1726, Henry Fielding's *Tom Jones* in 1749, Jane Austen's *Sense and Sensibility* in 1811, and *Pride and Prejudice* in 1813. The popularity of these novels, which portray individual moral struggles in matters such as religion, patriotism, love, and civic duty reveals a nation made up of individuals consistently concerned to work out for themselves the right thing to do.

The liberal civilisation we have evolved is intimately tied in with the power to govern our own affairs. If our capacity for self-government is allowed to drain away to Brussels, then our government will simply lack the ability to uphold our distinctive tradition of personal freedom. The importance of retaining control of the power of government has been powerfully demonstrated by studies that seek to understand why some nations are rich and others poor. Average income tends to be much higher in countries with accountable governments whose aim is to encourage an inclusive society in which everyone has a fighting chance of success. Nations run by unaccountable elites largely for their own benefit tend to be poor. The exceptions are nations with natural resources, especially oil, that allow the rulers to keep social peace without ceding political control to their citizens. This is powerfully demonstrated by Paul Collier's[46] study of the 'bottom billion', but with even greater clarity in the book *Why Nations Fail*. The authors use the small town of Nogales on the US/Mexican border to explain the consequences of having a democratic government accountable to the electorate as opposed to being ruled by what they call an 'extractive elite'.

Nogales is divided by a fence, with roughly half the town in Mexico and half in the US state of Arizona. The average household income in the American half is $30,000, whereas over the fence it is about one-third of that figure. Because they are elected, the various levels of US government provide health care, schools, good roads, sewers and law and order. On the Mexican side, there is far more crime, worse health care, poorer roads, and inadequate schools. People who might set up businesses are less confident that the results of any hard work will not simply be stolen. Moreover, setting up a business involves paying bribes to officials. In America the government actively supports institutions that allow people to use their time and energy to provide goods and services and achieve prosperity through hard work. There is occasional corruption in America, but the people know that the government is in a real sense their agent. They can weed out any serious wrongdoers. In America, even the most cynical and calculating politician will find that the best way to keep office is to provide citizens with the services they want. This is simply not true of Mexico.[47]

There are elections, but they do not provide an opportunity for the citizens to pressurise political leaders into promoting an inclusive society with opportunity for all.

Americans are more prosperous because their political system creates the structure which makes it realistic to believe that anyone can succeed by their own exertions. The sentiment is sometimes expressed in the extreme form that anyone can become anything they want. It's not literally true but it is correct to claim that you will never know how successful you could be unless you try. In a country ruled by an extractive elite, rather than a government that is the agent of the people, it is not worth exerting yourself to the same extent.

The European Commission is not an extractive elite in this sense, but it is an elite bent on centralising power at the expense of member nations. It undermines the solidarity and potential for give-and-take that enables people of all classes and interests to maintain confidence that the government is their ally, and not the instrument of a powerful group with interests separate from their own.

2

What Have We Lost?
Key Political and Constitutional
Developments

Our system of government by consent emerged from centuries of struggle to retain the advantages of government without allowing rulers to do whatever they pleased. From time to time in our history, kings who misused their powers were overthrown, but after the last such revolution in 1688, the government of the day ceased to be the monarch. Having suffered at the hands of absolutist rulers, the British people resolved that future governments were to be committees drawn from parliament that could rule only so long as they had the support of the House of Commons. A government that lost a vote of no confidence by MPs had to resign and face an immediate general election. It took centuries to evolve this system but since 1973, when we joined the European Economic Community, our ability to remove the real wielders of power has been weakened.

Our greatest constitutional historians, including F.W. Maitland of Cambridge University and Edward Freeman of Oxford, concur that by the reign of Edward I (1272-1307) the main features of our constitution were established. The key institutions were the king; an assembly of clergy, lords and commons; a king's council; the high offices of state, such as the chancellor; and the courts of law. Parliaments of the fourteenth century exercised all the powers of more recent parliaments: they dismissed ministers, regulated the royal household, and deposed kings from time to time. But, as the Tudor and Stuart regimes showed, our constitutional traditions were not out of danger until the revolution of 1688 ended the absolutism of monarchs permanently.[1]

An elected king?

The origins of the system lie in Anglo-Saxon times, and the Saxons seem to have been typical of the Germanic tribes described by Tacitus in the first century AD.[2] An assembly elected a king from those of noble descent, and assigned him only limited powers. In England the assembly was the witenagemot, whose membership seems to have varied. It was not a popular assembly but a gathering of 'the wise', including bishops and ealdormen. Before 1066, the assembly had significant power, including the right to elect and depose the king, to legislate along with the king, to give counsel and consent to laws, to nominate bishops and ealdormen jointly with the king, to grant public lands and taxes, and to declare peace and war. It was also a tribunal of last resort for civil and criminal law.[3] Maitland's assessment was that the most admirable element in the Anglo-Saxon constitution was 'that as yet no English king has taken on himself to legislate or to tax without the counsel and consent of a national assembly'.[4]

Before 1066 kings were elected from among the members of noble families, including the last two Anglo-Saxon kings, Edward and Harold. William I based his claim to the throne on his nomination by Edward the Confessor, but the power of a king to name his successor was not recognised by the witenagemot. War followed and William won, but despite taking the Crown by force he subsequently sought the support of the assembly. He was asked to swear an oath to uphold the laws of Edward the Confessor, as did later Norman kings. The death of the Conqueror led to fighting between his sons, Robert and William Rufus, and the approval of the witenagemot was used to legitimise the succession of the younger son, William. These Norman rulers were dictators but they governed with the counsel and consent of the barons, thus preserving something of the Anglo-Saxon tradition.[5] Gradually over many decades, the authoritarianism of the Normans was replaced by a system more fully resembling Anglo-Saxon conventions.

By the time of Edward I (1272-1307) the crown was being treated as hereditary, but before then kings had not been able to rely on hereditary right. In addition to William Rufus, Henry I, Stephen and John were elected. But Henry III, Edward I, II and III and Richard II followed in line of descent. However, Edward II and Richard II were deposed.[6]

The emergence of parliament

The first recorded example of local parliamentary representatives being called to a meeting occurred in 1213, when King John summoned four lawful men from each shire to an assembly in Oxford. The membership of the 'national assembly' was identified for the first time two years later in the Magna Carta.[7] Under Henry III (1216-1272) the powers of parliament grew, primarily when demands by Henry for money were met by demands from the assembly for reform. The struggle for supremacy came to a head between 1258 and 1265, when the rebel forces led by Simon de Montfort were defeated at Evesham. Despite that setback, by the end of the thirteenth century a recognisable parliament existed.[8]

What was the legal status of the king in the thirteenth century? Bracton, a judge for 20 years under Henry III, accepted that the king could not be sued or punished, but was not above the law: 'The king is below no man, but he is below God and the law; law makes the king; the king is bound to obey the law, though if he break it, his punishment must be left to God.' Although the king could not be brought before a court, the common opinion in the thirteenth and fourteenth centuries was that a king who would not rule according to law could be deposed. There was no legal machinery for deposition, as events in 1327 and 1399 show, which in Maitland's view effectively meant that there was 'a right of revolt, a right to make war upon your king'.[9]

The parliament of 1327 felt it had the power to depose an unworthy ruler such as Edward II, but the removal of Richard II in 1399 was of greater constitutional significance. He was explicitly removed for assuming absolute powers not recognised by the English people. Charges of breaking the law were drawn up against him. He had made laws without parliament, and treated private lives and property as if they were at his personal disposal. He was deposed in favour of Henry IV and compelled to sign a deed of abdication.[10]

Richard II had tried to rule as an absolute monarch but his attempt had been rejected. The House of Lancaster ruled from 1399 and is associated with strong parliamentary rule. Sir John Fortescue served the Lancastrians as chief justice and said repeatedly that the king was not an absolute monarch. In one of his most important works, he contrasted England with France, where the ruler was a dictator with unlimited power. Henry V (1413-1422), for example, was a popular king, but when he tried to name his successor, parliament denied him the right to dispose of the kingdom.[11]

A few years later, however, the power of parliament was threatened by the Yorkists during the Wars of the Roses. They asserted the right to rule in defiance of statute. Edward IV seized the throne by force in 1461 and parliament felt compelled to recognise him. Eventually, the Tudors took the throne in 1485 and by 1509, when Henry VII died, the king's powers were clearly defined. He summoned parliament and he could prorogue parliament. He could create peers, nominate bishops, and grant boroughs the right to send representatives to parliament. If elections were disputed, the issue was resolved by the king and his council. These entitlements gave him great influence on the membership of parliament. Moreover, the king's assent was necessary to law; and he could make ordinances. But he could not impose a tax, repeal a statute, or interfere with the ordinary courts of justice. He was bound by law. He could personally do no wrong and could not be sued in a court, but his power was checked by requiring the king to carry out all official tasks through servants who could be sued, dismissed or impeached. The king was the head of the government, but he did not have exclusive control over all executive functions. Parliament took an interest in many details. Some taxes were earmarked, and royal accounts had to be produced and audited. Offices were held during the king's pleasure, but sometimes parliament dictated who his office holders should be.[12]

Despite these limits, during Tudor and Stuart times progress towards government by consent went backwards. Henry VIII frequently used parliament as a mere reflection of his will. It passed bills of attainder whenever he wished and enforced whatever religious beliefs the king preferred. However, it suited Henry VIII to observe the letter of the law. Other foreign kings at the time abolished or ignored their national assemblies but Henry showed formal respect and, despite perverting the law and parliament, his retention of outward forms made it easier to restore free institutions in the seventeenth century.[13]

Tudor and Stuart monarchs argued that parliament owed its authority to the king; while others argued that parliament was the legitimate final authority with or without the king's approval. Freeman showed that the Glorious Revolution of 1688 restored the traditional position. For many centuries it had been claimed that parliament was automatically dissolved on the death of the king, and so had no authority without the king. Parliament was indeed summoned by the king's writ, but in the eleventh century kings such as Edward the Confessor and Harold had been elected after their predecessor had died. The assembly was needed most when the crown was vacant and someone had to decide how to fill it. The same was true when the next in line was a child, too young to rule. Parliament had appointed a regent when Henry III succeeded to the throne at the age of nine, and had appointed a Lord Protector, when Henry VI became king at the age of only nine months. In practice, calling parliament by means of a royal writ was a convenient way of assembling parliament and no more. The right of the people to meet and decide did not depend on the king issuing a summons. According to Freeman, in the eleventh century, 'it was not the king who created the assembly, but the assembly which created the king'.

The truth of his contention was confirmed in 1660, when the Convention Parliament recalled Charles II.

Contrary to what some legal theorists claimed, the Long Parliament did not end in 1649 when Charles I was executed. It was recalled in 1660, when it proceeded to choose a king and grant him a revenue. For the sake of form, its decisions were confirmed under a new Convention Parliament, but the work of selecting Charles II had already been done.[14]

The events of 1688 left no doubt about the supremacy of parliament over the king. An irregular assembly of parliamentarians from the reign of Charles II met in December 1688 to depose James II and elect William and Mary. It was claimed that James II had abdicated when he fled the country, but in truth he was forced from office. These events show that it had long been accepted that in times of revolution parliament could be called without a royal writ. By 1688 the doctrine was that parliament should be summoned by writ, but, according to Freeman, 'it was not from that summons, but from the choice of the people, that parliament derives its real being and its inherent powers'.[15]

The irregular meeting of 1688 advised the prospective new king to call a new Convention Parliament, which met in January 1689. It resolved that James II had subverted his contract with the people, and had abdicated leaving the throne vacant. It formally offered the crown to William and Mary. The Convention Parliament was not dissolved until March 1690 and went on to pass the bill of rights.[16]

Freeman's interpretation showed that every act to restrain the arbitrary prerogatives of the crown was a return to the spirit of our earlier law, not only before the Conquest, but as it had developed in the thirteenth century and especially during its Lancastrian heyday in the fifteenth century.[17] No one was king until he had been called forth by the assembly and anointed by the Church.

There are strong counter-arguments. From the Conquest it is true that the idea of hereditary right grew and 'men gradually came to look on kingship as a possession held by a single man for his own profit, rather than as an office bestowed by the people for the common good of the realm'.[18] Moreover, much confusion was caused by Blackstone, who wrongly claimed that kings had not been elected. His mistake was repeated by subsequent authors. But the facts reveal the opposite. As Edward II, Richard II, Charles I and James II discovered when they tried to act like dictators, an English king received his right to reign from the people. Moreover, when Charles II was invited from exile to serve as King of England, he was trusted with a limited power, to govern by and according to the laws of the land and not otherwise. He, like all his predecessors, was 'responsible to the Commons of England'.[19]

Rule by lawyers

So far we have been concerned about the relative power of the king and parliament, and by 1689 the victory of parliament was complete. But there was another rival for power that came to prominence in the early seventeenth century. Maitland describes the period as a fight between three rivals for final power: the king alone, the king in parliament, and the law as declared by lawyers.[20]

For a brief period, lawyers made a bid for supremacy. They failed, and perhaps their ambitions would not matter much to us if it were not for the fact that human-rights lawyers are using the same ploy to gain supremacy today.

Sir Edward Coke, chief justice for a time under James I, thought that the common law was above statute and above the royal prerogative. Judges, he argued, could hold a statute void on two grounds: first, when they considered it to be against reason or natural (divine) law; or second, if it infringed the royal prerogative. Coke cites precedents but Maitland found them unconvincing. Judges of the middle ages, Maitland showed, did not think they could question statutes in the belief that they were against natural law. It is true that, under James I, judges did claim the right to declare that a statute was not valid law. Bonham's Case of 1610 is the landmark ruling. Dr Bonham was a medical doctor educated at the University of Cambridge who started to practise in London in 1606. The College of Physicians had been chartered by an Act of Parliament that gave it the sole right to license individuals to practise medicine in London. The College refused to license Dr Bonham and when he continued to practise he was fined £5. He carried on treating patients and the College arrested him, at which point Dr Bonham sued for false imprisonment. Coke, sitting in the Court of Common Pleas, ruled that the Act of Parliament gave the College the right to issue licences in order to protect its monopoly and not for the benefit of the public. Moreover, when it fined and imprisoned Dr Bonham it was acting as a judge in its own cause, contrary to common law. Coke concluded that, under the authority of the common law, the courts could declare the relevant Act of Parliament void.[21]

When ruling that the College could not act as a judge in its own cause, he said: 'And it appeareth in our Books, that in many cases, the common law doth control Acts of Parliament, and sometimes shall adjudge them to be void: for when an Act of Parliament is against common right and reason, or repugnant, or impossible to be performed, the common law will control it, and adjudge such an Act to be void.'[22]

Judges did not expressly claim the power to legislate, only that the law—common law and natural law—had an existence of its own, independent of the will of any person. The law of nature (sometimes referred to as natural law) and the common law are occasionally treated as if they are the same thing, but in English legal tradition they are very different. The common law is the name for laws enforced by the courts of England, especially since the reign of Henry II (1154-1189) who introduced a national (common) system of courts, whereas the law of nature was considered to pre-date common law and to represent a higher standard than any human law. It was God's law.

A clear statement is found in one of the most important cases in the seventeenth century, Calvin's case of 1608. It was heard by all the judges of England, including Sir Edward Coke, chief justice of the Court of Common Pleas. It concerned Robert Calvin, a Scot who acquired land in England. Normally an alien could not own land, and his property was seized by Richard and Nicholas Smith. Calvin argued that he was born three years after King James VI of Scotland became King James I of England and consequently was not an alien.

The judges found that the allegiance of the subject was due to the King by the 'law of nature'; that the law of nature was part of the law of England; that the law of nature was 'before any judicial or municipal law'; and that the law of nature was 'immutable' or eternal.[23] Calvin was, therefore, entitled to own the property.

In his 'Reports' Coke describes the law of nature as 'that which God at the time of creation of the nature of man infused into his heart, for his preservation and direction'. This law had been 'written with the finger of God in the heart of man' and the 'people of God' had been governed by it before the law of Moses, which was considered to be the first written law.[24]

The natural 'obedience of the subject to the Sovereign cannot be altered'. Such obedience was due 'many thousand years before any law of man was made'.[25] The laws of nature were 'most perfect and immutable, whereas the condition of human law always runs into the infinite and there is nothing in them which can stand for ever'. Human laws were 'born, live and die'.[26]

Maitland, however, points out that this doctrine had never been a working doctrine. In the fourteenth, fifteenth and sixteenth centuries, for example, parliament had made laws about virtually everything and had not recognised any theory of law above the king or parliament.[27] And the supremacy of common law, divine law or natural law, was not subsequently accepted by parliament. The fount of legitimacy was the king in parliament.

Rule by the king alone or the king in parliament

The seventeenth century fixed sovereignty with the king in parliament and not with the king alone. Moreover, no permanent power by kings to make proclamations had been recognised for long. In 1539 an Act had been passed (the Statute of Proclamations) saying that the king could make proclamations with the advice of his council and that such proclamations had the force of statutes. Breaches could be punished by fine or prison, but not life, limb or forfeiture. The Act was, however, repealed in 1547 under Edward VI, which demonstrated that the king in parliament (not the king alone) was supreme. Powers could be given and they could be taken back. Parliament cannot bind its successors. Tyranny can be undone.

Nevertheless, the Stuart kings maintained that they had a right to issue proclamations. The claimed power was put to the test under James I. In 1610 Coke was asked if a royal proclamation could prevent the building of houses in London and prohibit the making of starch from wheat. He and three other senior judges found that no proclamation could cancel a law or create a new one, but that the king could admonish by proclamation his subjects to obey existing laws.[28]

James I and Charles I ignored this legal advice and used the Court of Star Chamber to enforce their commands, until it was abolished by the Long Parliament in 1641. According to Maitland, Star Chamber was a court of politicians enforcing a policy, not a court of judges administering law, words that could be applied to the European Court of Justice today.

However, the king had always been permitted to dispense with laws in particular cases. Dispensing was closely connected with pardoning or declining to prosecute a case, perhaps because it was not in the public interest. The king was said to have been wronged by breaches of law, and if he chose not to prosecute, so be it. But this power to dispense with the law in the case of particular individuals is not to be confused with the power claimed by some kings to suspend statutes. The bill of rights in 1689 ended suspension totally. The matter had been brought to a head in 1687 by James II's 'declaration of indulgence' that suspended all punitive laws against non-conformists and Catholics. The bill of rights pronounced in unambiguous words that the 'pretended power' of suspension was illegal.[29]

It had long been accepted that the king could not impose a tax without the approval of parliament. However, kings unable to gain parliamentary support for taxation had tried numerous other devices, including forced loans and compulsory gifts from wealthy individuals. The Tudors had raised money by granting monopolies covering vital commodities like salt, leather and coal. They were unpopular because prices tended to rise, and in 1597 the Commons began to protest. In 1601 Elizabeth had promised not to create more monopolies, but the practice continued under later kings.

Parliament sought to increase its control of all sources of revenue and demanded that kings must seek the approval of parliament, not only to raise taxes but also to raise revenue in other ways. The Petition of Right in 1628 put severe limits on the ability of Charles I to resort to alternative revenues by stipulating that no one could be forced to make a gift or loan, or pay a tax without the agreement of parliament. Charles assented but then ignored the law by running the country from 1629-1640 without calling a parliament. The 'ship money' case of 1634 brought matters to a head. The king ordered coastal and inland towns to pay a tax to cover the cost of ships. The great parliamentarian, John Hampden, refused to pay and the court of Exchequer-Chamber was required to rule. By a vote of 7-5 it found against Hampden. Some of the judges even ruled that the king's proclamations were laws. The king's power, they thought, was absolute. He was wise to consult his people, but it was only a moral obligation. However, when the Long Parliament was finally called, it declared the judgement void in 1641.[30]

Not only did parliament try to control the king's revenue, it also sought to control expenditure. Under Henry IV, parliament had forced the king to render accounts. Under the Tudors the practice stopped, but in 1641 parliament required accounts from Charles I. After the Restoration of 1660, parliament became even more determined. In 1665 it made money available for the Dutch war, but insisted that it must only be applied to the war and demanded accounts to show where the money had gone. After the revolution of 1688 it was accepted that the Treasury was required to spend only as parliament had agreed. A further important stage in parliamentary control came in 1698 when the civil list, allocating income for the king's personal use, was approved. A primary aim had been to put limits on the ability of the king to bribe MPs with salaries and pensions.[31]

In addition to gaining control of the Crown, the House of Commons also sought to limit the power of the Lords. Increasingly it was felt that the House of Lords should not have an equal say with the Commons on the taxation of the people. Under Charles II, in 1661 and 1671 it was accepted that 'money bills' must be initiated in the Commons and not amended by the Lords. They must take them or leave them.

The independence of judges was also a vital element in avoiding dictatorship. English judges had always held office at 'the king's pleasure' and the majority in parliament wanted judges to hold office 'during good behaviour', so that they were not dependent on the king. However, William III refused to give ground and the issue was not settled until the Act of Settlement was passed. From 1701 judges could be removed on an address of both houses of parliament to the Crown. Judges no longer depended on royal favour but, just as important for their independence, they could not be removed on the whim of the Commons alone.[32]

Emergence of Cabinet government accountable to parliament

The Glorious Revolution set limits to the king's powers. He was below statute, had no power to suspend statutes, could not create a new legal offence by proclamation, and could not maintain an army without consent. Income could be earmarked for specific purposes, and judges held office on good behaviour, not at the king's pleasure. Special courts were not allowed.

The revolution, said Maitland, was a restoration of the ancient constitution as it stood under the Lancastrians. This meant that, under William and Mary, the king remained a governing king with a policy. William and Mary attended the Cabinet, which was legally a meeting of the privy council. It was only under George I and II that the monarch did not attend, chiefly because neither could speak English.[33]

As in earlier times, the sovereign was still not personally responsible if he committed crimes or misdemeanours, but his agents were. Before 1689 parliament had to impeach ministers, but after that date a vote of censure in the Commons was as effective as impeachment. Moreover, even when ministers were in no danger of prosecution or impeachment, they were no less bound to bow to the will of the House of Commons.[34] The House of Commons had, in practice, become the ruling power in the nation.

Ministers were in parliament as MPs or lords and had to answer questions. Committees of parliament could ask witnesses to testify on oath and reluctant individuals could be summoned for contempt if they would not attend.

From the reign of William III there was a recognisable ministry that acted with at least some coherence. Previously ministers were individual office holders under the Crown, but under Anne and George I, Cabinet solidarity begins to emerge. There is a single head, a political programme, and a common responsibility to parliament. Under Anne, both Whigs and Tories were in the Cabinet, but Robert Walpole (prime minister from 1721 to 1742) restricted membership to Whigs. Henceforward, ministers represented a party not a king.[35] The king was bound to act on the advice of ministers and had to choose ministers in accordance with the will of the Commons. High offices of state were held at the king's pleasure, but the monarch was required to choose a prime minister who commanded the confidence of the Commons and to appoint his nominees to office.

Officers of state who were not in the ministry also held office at the king's pleasure but had in fact become permanent civil servants. Normally they were not permitted to sit in the Commons or to play an active part in politics.[36]

By the nineteenth century political parties had become central, along with the idea of a loyal opposition. The existence of a rival government-in-waiting made the constitutional possibility of removing the government a realistic threat. One stumble by the ruling party, and another lot could take over without serious disruption. During the nineteenth century the franchise was gradually extended so that bit-by-bit the parties became more representative of the population, a process that was not completed until the twentieth century.

The twentieth century: the true political sovereign is the electorate

By the beginning of the twentieth century the main characteristics of our constitution had long been clear. One of the best statements of the longstanding view of the British people is still to be found in the 1915 edition of A.V. Dicey's *The Law of the Constitution*. According to Dicey, the vital distinction in our system was between 'legal' sovereignty and 'political' sovereignty:

> Parliament is, from a merely legal point of view, the absolute sovereign... since every Act of Parliament is binding on every Court... and no rule, whether of morality or of law, which contravenes an Act of Parliament binds any Court throughout the realm. But if Parliament be in the eye of the law a supreme legislature, the essence of representative government is, that the legislature should represent or give effect to the will of the political sovereign, i.e. of the electoral body, or of the nation.[37]

Dicey describes how our constitution was made up of both laws and conventions. There was 'the law of the constitution' – the enforceable laws that laid down constitutional principles – and the 'conventions of the constitution' – the habits and traditions that are observed but not directly enforced by law. The conventions had one ultimate object: 'to secure that Parliament, or the Cabinet which is indirectly appointed by Parliament, shall in the long run give effect to the will of that power which in modern England is the true political sovereign of the State – the majority of the electors or... the nation'.[38]

Dicey strongly maintains that 'the electorate is in fact the sovereign of England'. The whole people act through a 'supreme legislature' whose conduct is 'regulated by understandings of which the object is to secure the

44

conformity of Parliament to the will of the nation'. All the conventions that uphold the supremacy of the House of Commons in practice uphold the 'sovereignty of the people'.[39] To prove the point, Dicey examines three conventions: (1) the requirement that the powers of the Crown are exercised through ministers enjoying the confidence of Parliament; (2) the convention that the House of Lords gives way to the Commons; and (3) the right of kings to dissolve parliament against the wishes of the majority of MPs.

The rule that the powers of the Crown must be exercised through ministers who are members of the Commons or the Lords and who 'command the confidence of the House of Commons', in practice, means that the elected part of the legislature appoints the executive. It also means that ministers must ultimately carry out, 'or at any rate not contravene, the wishes of the House of Commons', which in turn means they must reflect the wishes of the electorate as interpreted by MPs.[40]

The same is true of the convention that the House of Lords is expected in every serious political controversy to give way to the will of the House of Commons. At what point should the Lords give way, or should the Crown use its prerogative to create new peers? The guiding principle, said Dicey, is that the Lords must yield or the Crown intervene when it is conclusively shown that 'the House of Commons represents on the matter in dispute the deliberate decision of the nation'. And if the deliberate decision of the electorate is the vital consideration, then conventions guiding the House of Lords and the Crown are rules 'meant to ensure the ultimate supremacy of the true political sovereign', the electorate.[41]

Dicey also shows how the right of the Crown to dissolve parliament affirms the political sovereignty of the people. At first glance this power looks like a continuation of earlier royal absolutism, but as Dicey put it, the reason why the House can in accordance with the constitution be dissolved 'is that an occasion has arisen on which there is fair reason to suppose that the opinion of the House is not the opinion of the electors'. In such cases dissolution is in its essence 'an appeal from the legal to the political sovereign'. A dissolution is allowable 'whenever the wishes of the legislature are, or may fairly be presumed to be, different from the wishes of the nation'.[42]

He gives as examples the dissolutions of 1784 and 1834. In December 1783, George III dismissed the government of Charles James Fox and Lord North and installed an administration led by Pitt the Younger. Pitt did not have the support of the Commons and the king dissolved parliament, leading to an election in March 1784. The result vindicated his decision and Pitt's administration was returned. The precedent was established that the Cabinet, when supported by the king (who has the power of dissolution), can 'defy the will of a House of Commons if the House is not supported by the electors'. The fundamental principle was that 'the legal sovereignty of Parliament is subordinate to the political sovereignty of the nation'.[43]

In December 1834 the king replaced Melbourne's Whig administration with one led by Peel. He dissolved parliament, but the election in 1835 went strongly against Peel's administration and the Whigs returned soon afterwards. According to Dicey, the essential point in both 1784 and 1834 was that 'it is the verdict of the political sovereign' or nation that ultimately determines the right of a Cabinet to retain office.[44] The supremacy of the electorate was reaffirmed in 1841, when Peel moved a motion of no confidence against Melbourne. It was carried by only one vote, but an election was required. The majority in the Commons did not think the policy of the ministry was beneficial to the nation and so the government was obliged to resign.[45]

All the conventions of the constitution, according to Dicey, were 'intended to secure the ultimate supremacy of the electorate as the true political sovereign of the State'. Constitutional maxims are 'subordinate and subservient to the fundamental principle of popular sovereignty'.[46]

The Coalition Government that took office in 2010 has convinced itself that it has introduced fixed-term parliaments, but the 2011 Fixed-Term Parliaments Act provides for elections to be held before five years have elapsed if the House of Commons passes a vote of no confidence in the Government or if a motion is approved by two-thirds of the House of Commons. It is a fundamental constitutional principle of our system that no Parliament can bind its successors, for the obvious reason that it must be possible for injustices, or self-serving political decisions, to be rectified immediately. However, the act also stipulates that 'Parliament cannot otherwise be dissolved', which appears to abolish the power of the Queen to call an election if she believes that the Government lacks the support of the people.

Before turning to the impact of the 1972 European Communities Act on our constitution, a few words about historical interpretation are necessary. Some historians have made a concerted effort to deny that the people of Britain have been engaged in a long struggle for freedom and democracy, a view they denounce as 'Whig history'.

Whig history

Some commentators contend that describing our national story as a long struggle that ended in the achievement of constitutional liberalism is 'Whig history', which they consider to be a very bad thing. Simon Schama described the pressure he felt from critics of 'Whig history' when he was producing his book and TV series, *A History of Britain*. Historians such as Macaulay were treated as if they lived: 'in a world drained of historical free will, of the uncertainty of outcomes, a past ordered to march in lock-step to the drumbeat of the Protestant, parliamentary future'. However, Schama found that on looking afresh at British history there was a lot of truth in the Whig claim that the partial success of the 'party of liberty represented a genuine turning point in the political history of the world'. Schama defiantly declared that if, by concluding that much of the Whig story was true, he had revealed himself as 'that most hopeless anachronism, a born-again Whig, so be it'.[47]

Among Schama's accusers were David Cannadine, who has said that Whig history was:

> fiercely partisan and righteously judgemental, dividing the personnel of the past into the good and the bad. And it did so on the basis of the marked preference for liberal and progressive causes, rather than conservative and reactionary ones... Whig history was, in short, an extremely biased view of the past: eager to hand out moral judgements, and distorted by teleology, anachronism and present-mindedness.[48]

Another accuser is Norman Davies in his book *The Isles* where he says that:

> Once the Whigs had triumphed in that 'Glorious Revolution' of 1688-89, their view of history triumphed with them. Everything that happened prior to 1688 was to be viewed teleologically as tending towards that glorious achievement.[49]

Davies focuses his critical attention on a study by a Frenchman, Paul Rapin de Thoyras, published between 1726 and 1731, which contained the Whig interpretation 'in a nutshell'. However, Hume's *History of England*, published from 1754 to 1762, gave a 'huge impetus' to the Whig interpretation, even though Davies admits that Hume was 'no political partisan and he was not a practising Protestant'. Nevertheless, Hume's optimistic account gave the impression that: 'Protestantism, the Union, and the Empire were all moving serenely in the right general direction'.[50] Davies' hostility to England and her achievements made it impossible for his mind to entertain the possibility that the non-partisan Hume had simply spoken the truth.

Davies is one of those writers who understands that to undermine an established order you have to break the sense of allegiance that binds its members. If they are united and loyal to their national system of liberal democracy, then the national story must be challenged and another one substituted. The people of England cannot be allowed to take pride in the achievements of their ancestors in struggling for freedom and democracy, their story is one of exploitation of the weak by the strong. Democracy is a disguise for the real interests that dominate. Davies gives the impression of wanting to destroy our national solidarity in order to create the space in which to build a new kind of 'national' allegiance, to the EU.

Accusing people of believing in the Whig inter-pretation of history has proved to be very useful, not least because of the ambiguity of the accusation. Sometimes the Whig interpretation is criticised by historians because they do not like to look back on events to understand the present. Rather, they think we should try to get inside the minds of individuals in earlier ages to see things as they appeared to them in their own day. This was one of the concerns of Herbert Butterfield, the academic whose essay of 1931 'The Whig interpretation of history' first sparked the dispute. He wrote:

> It is part and parcel of the Whig interpretation of history that it studies the past with reference to the present. ... On this system the historian is bound to construe his function as demanding him to be vigilant for likenesses between past and present, instead of being vigilant for unlikeness; so that he will find it easy to say that he has seen the present in the past, he will imagine that he has discovered a 'root' or an 'anticipation' of the twentieth century, when in reality he is in a world of different connotations altogether, and he has merely tumbled upon what could be shown to be a misleading analogy. ... The Whig interpretation of history is not merely the property of Whigs and it is much more subtle than mental bias; it lies in a trick of organization, an unexamined habit of mind that any historian may fall into. It is the result of the practice of abstracting things from their historical context and judging them apart from their context.[51]

He concluded:

> This is why Sir Walter Scott has helped us to understand the Covenanters, and Thomas Carlyle has made an important contribution to our estimate of Cromwell. The historian is something more than the mere passive external spectator. ... By imaginative sympathy he makes the past intelligible to the present. He translates its conditioning circumstances into terms which we today can understand.[52]

This approach, sometimes called history for its own sake, is often valid but it is not preferable to investigative objectivity as normally understood. Writing slightly before Butterfield in 1927, Julien Benda criticised intellectuals who adopted a pose of permanent impartiality – a 'frenzy of impartiality' as he called it. He has in mind French intellectuals who would not condemn German aggression in 1914 because, if they accepted that their country was right, they would lose their impartiality. Benda wrote ironically that they would have taken up the cause of France if it had not been their own country.[53] For them impartiality meant never taking sides. But scientific objectivity does not entail constantly sitting on the fence, it requires the investigator to go through a disinterested stage to discover the truth – and then to speak out without fear or favour.

Butterfield was concerned about historical methods, but today the accusation of 'Whig history' is primarily levelled as a weapon in the war of ideas over how we should understand ourselves in our own time. I have argued that our national story can accurately be described as a long struggle over the centuries to resist the absolute power of rulers and to create accountable government. Ultimately these developments led to liberal con-stitutionalism. Those who want to portray history as a story of the exploitation of the weak by the strong don't like this conclusion. But it seems to me that it is an objective fact. It is what a reasonable person would conclude after looking at the facts in a disinterested frame of mind, and after undergoing a period of scholarly doubt and self-criticism. Modern democracy puts the majority in control, subject to constitutional constraints.

Among the other accusations made against 'Whig historians' by recent writers like Cannadine is that they believed that progress was inevitable. Macaulay is often cited as a Whig historian (though not by Butterfield who targets Lord Acton and his famous essays on 'The History of Freedom in Antiquity' and 'The History of Freedom in

Christianity'). According to Butterfield: 'It might be true to say that in Lord Acton, the Whig historian reached his highest consciousness.'[54]

But is it true that Macaulay believed in the inevitability of the Whig mission? Looking back on the century and a half before 1848, Macaulay said: 'the history of our country during the last hundred and sixty years is eminently the history of physical, of moral, and of intellectual improvement.' The general effect of this 'chequered narrative' will be 'to excite thankfulness in all religious minds, and hope in the breasts of all patriots'.[55]

He was, therefore, pleased with what he found and optimistic about the future, but did he think that events had been inevitable? In fact, he was only too aware of how fragile had been the achievements of 1688 and 1689, the pivotal moment in the emergence of liberalism. He gives a blow by blow account of how the national debate ebbed back and forth. For example, the resolution to declare the throne vacant in 1688 was hotly contested in the House of Lords. On one occasion the motion was rejected by 55 votes to 41.[56] The Commons, too, was divided. In one vote on some Lords' amendments the House divided by 282 to 151. Eventually, however, the Lords voted by 62 to 47 in favour of appointing William and Mary in place of James II.

Moreover, when debating the conditions on which the throne was to be granted, the disagreements continued, even when the most vital issues were raised. Macaulay writes that during the discussion about the Declaration of Rights:

It is a most remarkable circumstance that, while the whole political, military, judicial, and fiscal system of the kingdom was thus passed in review, not a single representative of the people proposed the repeal of the statute which subjected the press to a censorship.[57]

And, as already described above, the independence of judges was not guaranteed until 1701. In addition, the religious toleration granted by the 1689 Act of Toleration was only limited. The Test Act continued to prevent Catholics, Protestant non-conformists, Jews and Unitarians from serving in Parliament. No one who reads Macaulay with the objectivity that we ought to be able to expect from professional historians could properly accuse Macaulay of treating events as if the final outcome had been inevitable.

After 1973

The UK joined the EEC on 1 January 1973, under the terms of the 1972 European Communities Act. Formally, the constitution described by Dicey remains in being. The electorate is the 'political sovereign'. But in practice power has slipped away to the institutions of the EU, and now many of our laws are effectively made in Brussels. Often Brussels enacts Directives, which have to be incorporated into national laws by each member state, but the true lawmaker in such cases is the European Union, not the nation state. As we learned the hard way during the long centuries of growing up as a free people, the essence of a democratic system is to be able to dismiss the government of the day and demand an immediate election whenever there is good reason for supposing that the government does not reflect the views of the majority. Public opinion may find its voice in the Commons, which can pass a vote of no confidence; or it can be represented by the Crown, which can dissolve parliament and trigger an election. Dicey's examples of the king dismissing the government are from the nineteenth century or earlier, but the same power has been exercised in modern times. Under the Australian constitution the powers of the monarch are exercised by the governor-general. In the 1970s the government of Gough Whitlam had lost the confidence of the Australian people and was removed by the governor-general so that an election could be held. The governor-general's decision was vindicated by the general election, which returned a different government with a large majority.

This precious ability to trigger an immediate election has not been formally lost, but it matters a lot less when parliament no longer makes all our laws and when much of the executive power lies in Brussels. The EU now has legal supremacy across many fundamental areas of our national life, a fact recognised by our courts.

Under British constitutional conventions, a government cannot change the law by signing a treaty. It must incorporate the terms of the treaty in law by an Act of Parliament. The 1957 Treaty of Rome was incorporated into UK law by the European Communities Act of 1972. Section 1 lists the treaties to which it applies and gives the government an extraordinary power to add new treaties to the list by an Order in Council. In effect it can override UK law by using the prerogative power claimed by monarchs but strenuously resisted for hundreds of years except for a brief period under Henry VIII.

Under section 2(1) all laws of the EEC that were directly applicable were immediately enforceable and were to prevail over future Acts of Parliament, if they were inconsistent with them.

Section 2(2) provided a general power to cover European regulations that did not have direct effect but required member states to make legal changes to implement them (such as measures following directives that allowed some room for national interpretation). Section 2(4) provided for future UK legislation. It stipulated that an Act passed after the 1972 Act that contradicted it would not be enforceable by the English courts. It contradicted the longstanding constitutional tradition that it is always open to a future parliament to reverse earlier mistakes or improve earlier legislation.[58]

Even these open-ended clauses did not give the EU bureaucracy the arbitrary power it sought. The Maastricht Treaty of 1992[59] contained article 308: 'If action by the Community should prove necessary to obtain, in the course of the operation of the common market, one of the objectives of the community and this Treaty has not provided the necessary powers, the council shall take the appropriate measures.'[60]

Where does final power lie in the event of a clash between Acts of Parliament and EU law? Lord Denning commented in 1976 that once a bill 'is passed by Parliament and becomes a statute, that will dispose of all discussion about the Treaty. These courts will then have to abide by the statute without regard to the Treaty at all.'[61]

However, in 1979 he took a very different line: 'In construing our statute, we are entitled to look at the Treaty as an aid to its construction: and even more, not only as an aid but as an overriding force.' If on close investigation our legislation is deficient then, under section 2 of the 1972 Act, 'it is our bounden duty to give priority to Community law'.[62]

Nevertheless, he provided for the possibility that Parliament might decide to reverse the 1972 Act:

> Thus far I have assumed that our Parliament, whenever it passes legislation, intends to fulfil its obligations under the

Treaty. If the time should come when our Parliament deliberately passes an Act – with the intention of repudiating the Treaty or any provision of it – or intentionally acting inconsistently with it – and says so in express terms – then I should have thought that it would be the duty of our courts to follow the statute of our Parliament.[63]

The greatest modern authority on the constitution, Sir William Wade, described the supremacy of the European Court of Justice as a constitutional revolution, by which he meant a new 'political fact' declaring where ultimate power was to be found.[64] He was prompted to make his claim by the final House of Lords decision in the Factortame case in 1990, which concerned the right to fish in British waters. The Merchant Shipping Act of 1894 had permitted foreign vessels to register as if they were British owned, thus permitting them to fish in our waters. By the 1980s some 95 Spanish vessels had registered and the British government was concerned that over-fishing was leading to the depletion of fish stocks. Parliament passed the Merchant Shipping Act in 1988 to require stronger proof of nationality. The 95 Spanish ships could not meet the new tests and a company called Factortame sought an injunction in the British courts ruling that the 1988 Act was contrary to EU law. The case eventually reached the House of Lords and in 1990 Lord Bridge gave the judgement, which found that EU law was superior to the 1988 Act and allowed the Spanish fishermen to continue fishing in British waters. He noted that there had been public criticism that the decision involved a 'novel and dangerous invasion' of the sovereignty of Parliament, but claimed that such comments were based on a misconception:

If the supremacy within the European Community of Community law over the national law of member states was not always inherent in the EEC Treaty (Cmnd. 5179-11) it was certainly well established in the jurisprudence of the European Court of Justice long before the United Kingdom joined the Community. Thus, whatever the limitation of its sovereignty Parliament accepted when it enacted the European Communities Act 1972 was entirely voluntary. Under the terms of the Act of 1972 it has always been clear that it was the duty of a United Kingdom court, when delivering final judgement, to override any rule of national law found to be in conflict with any directly enforceable rule of Community law.[65]

The supremacy of European over British law is clear enough and it remains to be seen what will happen if Parliament decides to pass an Act that deliberately contradicts European law.

But what about parliamentary scrutiny of the executive? The European Commission has far greater powers to ignore parliament than most of our kings. There has been very limited parliamentary scrutiny of European law. In 1972 the government expressed the view that: 'Parliament should be informed about and have an opportunity to consider at the formative stage those Community instruments which, when made by the Council, will be binding in this country.'[66]

In 1974 both Houses set up special committees to scrutinise legislation, the Commons Select Committee on European Scrutiny and the European Union Committee in the Lords. It has long been accepted that they do not provide adequate oversight. As early as 1978, the Commons Procedure Committee pointed out: 'the ability of the House to influence the legislative decisions of the Communities is inhibited by practical as well as legal and procedural obstacles'. There was inadequate time, national parliaments had no right to be consulted, and there was no control of legislation made by the Commission on its own authority.[67]

Twenty years later in 1998 Parliament stipulated that no minister of the Crown should agree to 'any proposal for European Community legislation': which was (a) still subject to scrutiny (that is, when the European Scrutiny Committee had not completed its examination); or (b) awaiting consideration by the House. However, these requirements could be waived in certain cases, including if there were 'special reasons'. In such cases, the minister was expected to explain the reasons to the European Scrutiny Committee and in some cases the House.[68]

A few MPs and peers have become very well informed about European issues, and some campaigners have stood their ground for the British constitution, including Conservative MP William Cash, Labour MP Austin Mitchell in the Commons and Lords Pearson, Stoddart and Vinson in the Lords. But the truth is that countless regulations whose future effects can only be guessed at are routinely forced into law after the barest examination by Parliament.

3

Why Independence Matters and How We Lost Our Way

Membership of the EU endangers our ability to preserve and develop our tradition of freedom and responsibility: not only the accountability of government to its citizens, but also the ability of public opinion to deploy the powers of government to foster personal freedom and opportunity. In our system of accountable government under the law, citizens are clear where our freedoms end. This legal certainty is especially important as a means of making it easier for strangers to co-exist and cooperate in civil society. But because so many of our laws are no longer made by Parliament, public opinion and free discussion now matter far less. The EU has the power to impose policies not wanted by our government and not supported by the majority of the British people.

Democracy of the kind we have nurtured in Britain requires a *demos* – a free people conscious of itself, owing allegiance to one another, seeking the common good, respectful of legitimate differences, and unified in a desire to give everyone a fighting chance. The EU's 'Euro-barometer' survey of public opinion sometimes asks whether people identify most with the region in which they live, their nation, Europe, or whether they feel 'citizens of the world'. In 2009, 94 per cent identified with their nationality, 91 per cent with their region, 74 per cent with Europe, and 64 per cent with citizenship of the world. There does not appear to be a more recent survey, but in 2013 Eurobarometer asked people whether they felt they were 'a citizen of the EU'. About 62 per cent said 'yes', but only 22 per cent replied 'yes, definitely', and 40 per cent replied 'yes, to some extent'. There were considerable differences between countries, but only four had a majority who did not feel they were citizens of the EU. The four included Britain, where only 48 per cent replied 'yes'.[1]

People have good reason for identifying with their nation. Genuine democracy is only attainable when those who are governed feel enough in common to accept the law of the land, and to acquiesce in peaceful transfers of power from one political party to another. National loyalty is assumed by democracy. The obligations we feel to one another allow space for freedom of speech, conscience and religion. They are no threat to our common loyalty. On the contrary, we learn from the clash of opinion.

Not only have we lost the ability to uphold our commitment to the free state as an engine for the development of personal abilities, we have also lost the means of dealing collectively with the special social and economic problems we face. A nation able to act collectively can make the most of the advantages and disadvantages of its territory and people. One nation may lack natural resources and have to overcome the problem by creating human or cultural capital. Singapore, for example, has few natural resources and has made up for it by shaping an excellent education system. Or a nation may have resources, which it seeks to conserve. Norway, for example, has made wise use of its oil reserves and fish stocks, not least by declining to join the EU. Ethnic and linguistic divisions in Switzerland, similar to those that have proved explosive elsewhere in Europe, have been overcome by means of a federal constitution that has allowed very different peoples to co-operate harmoniously. Canada, too, has avoided conflict between its English and French speaking communities by adopting a heavily decentralised system of government.

International trade is vitally important for the UK, and yet we have lost the ability to enter into trade agreements with non-EU nations. We are no longer separately represented at the World Trade Organisation and must instead accept the EU position. Management of monetary policy is another vital element in the success of a trading nation. Fortunately we did not join the euro and so do not suffer from the rigidities that have harmed the economies of countries such as Spain and Italy. It is particularly harmful that the eurozone denies its members the opportunity to allow the exchange rate to adjust to reflect unique national circumstances.

According to our constitution, no government or majority in parliament can deprive the next generation of the possibility of choosing their own way of life. But EU absolutism seeks to close down options. Shared or pooled sovereignty are deliberately deceitful terms that mean that outsiders can impose their preferences on us. Since we joined the EU, our ability to contribute to decision making has been severely weakened. From July 2013 the UK had 29 votes out of 352 in the Council of the European Union (8.2 per cent).[2] In 1973 the UK had held ten votes out of 58 (17.2 per cent), plus a veto over far more decisions. The UK's influence over the Commission has declined from two out of thirteen commissioners in 1973 to one out of 28 in 2013. And in the European Parliament, the UK had 81 out of 410 MEPs in 1979 (19.7 per cent) and only 73 out of 754 by 2012 (9.7 per cent).

It is sometimes said that globalisation has made nations less important because all are at the mercy of 'market forces', but it would be more true to say that globalisation has made the nation state more necessary.[3] The greater ability to travel, the use of the internet, and the easy movement of capital and goods that has been called 'globalisation' has made nation states more important, particularly to protect the casualties of change. Globalisation certainly puts constraints on what nation states can do, but that makes it all the more important for countries to keep what discretion they have. Whole industries can suddenly be hit by technological change with disastrous job losses. Switzerland, for example, has long been known for making watches. When digital watches were invented, traditional manufacturers lost thousands of jobs in a very short time. The Swiss government was able to step in and minimise the harm to displaced workers and ease the transition to alternatives. The German government has rescued Volkswagen in the past, the US government only recently bailed out its car industry, and the British government rescued some of our banks. Without national governments to provide a temporary respite, a downward economic spiral could easily affect all countries.

Moreover, many competitive advantages are created by governments. Often they are an historic achievement, or at least the result of policy decisions made decades earlier. American government investment in computers and electronics in the years after World War Two, for example, is still paying off today. One of the great disputes in recent decades has been about the extent to which governments should take direct responsibility for providing goods or services. In Britain, nationalisation was favoured for several decades after World War Two. Later, privatisation was pursued within a framework of laws designed to ensure competition. A people can decide that the government should aim to provide a legal framework for private provision of goods and services, or that the government should provide them through its departments or arms-length agencies. The approach can vary over time. Britain's rail track, for example, was privatised and then renationalised when private ownership failed. The recently nationalised banks are now being prepared for private sale. Nations need the space to make these judgments as circumstance's change. Getting permission from Brussels to change policy achieves little more than wasting time and adding to costs.

To summarise: the EU prevents nations from adapting to their unique circumstances. It is in the interests of all nations if each country makes the fullest use of its natural and human resources. But a nation is not just an economy, and the EU threatens, not only our economic prosperity, but also the elemental achievements of Britain's civilisation: our ability to act collectively for the common good through civil society as well as the state, and to ensure government by consent.

Why did we acquiesce in the abandonment of our own achievements?

Why have more voices not seen the danger as powers seeped away and the reality of the ambitions of the Brussels bureaucracy became more apparent? Among Conservatives, an important factor was a loss of self-confidence. They had been accustomed to Britain being a major player in world affairs and were badly demoralised by her manifest weakness after the exertions of the Second World War. The Suez crisis of 1956 was a tipping point and, as countries in the Empire were granted independence in the post-war years, many Tories looked to Europe as the source of alliances to bolster British security and prestige in the dangerous Cold-War era. But, instead of opting for alliances with nations that were prepared to respect one another's differences, they fell for the ploy of the zealots who wanted to construct a new international state at the expense of member nations. As a result, the Tory party contained many MPs who could no longer be counted on to be the champions of British independence. Alternative forms of cooperation were established with Britain's active involvement, including the Western European Union for common defence, EFTA for trade, and the Council of Europe, but they were to lose out to the EU. EFTA still exists but with only four members: Switzerland, Norway, Iceland and Liechtenstein. Only NATO remains as an effective framework for Europe-wide cooperation.

The Conservatives were also very conscious that the earliest members of the Common Market (as it was originally called in Britain) had enjoyed faster economic growth than the UK since World War II, and thought that joining it would increase our GDP. It was a grave misfortune that a bad situation was made worse when membership negotiations were led by the arrogant and deceitful Edward Heath, prime minister from 1970 to 1974, who willingly sacrificed British interests, such as our fishing industry. The best account of that period so far is *The Great Deception* by Christopher Booker and Richard North.[4]

Labour took office in 1974 and arranged a referendum in June 1975, but a large majority voted in favour of remaining in the EU. The main reason was that Britain's self-confidence had received a second blow. During the 1950s and 1960s most people became materially better off, but the 1970s brought a major economic crisis. The Bretton Woods era came to an end in 1971 when President

Nixon unilaterally ended the link between the dollar and gold. Until that time the dollar could be exchanged for gold at a fixed price and other major currencies could be exchanged for the dollar at fixed rates (subject to occasional devaluations or revaluations). Breaking the link between the dollar and gold led to high inflation in many countries and substantially reduced the revenues of oil-producing countries (oil was traded in dollars). They tried to push up the price of oil, leading to what became known as the 'first oil shock'. Over the winter of 1973-74 the problem was compounded by an oil embargo that resulted from the war between Israel and Egypt and Syria. The Americans sent arms to Israel and oil producers in OPEC cut off their supplies in retaliation.[5] In Britain, the first oil shock coincided with a miner's strike which led to the three-day week in January 1974. The stock market had crashed and between 1973 and 1975 UK GDP fell by over three per cent. Both inflation and unemployment increased sharply. The referendum took place in a crisis atmosphere in June 1975 and supporters of EU membership claimed that it would help Britain escape from its economic woes. The promise was a kind of escapism, but it worked.

Subsequently the two main parties have been internally divided. During the Thatcher years many in the Labour movement came to see the EU as an ally against Thatcherism in securing new workplace regulations and, paradoxically, many Thatcherites who were enthusiasts for free markets came to see the EU as an ally in removing regulatory barriers to trade.

Labour's divisions

The Labour party had traditionally been patriotic and strongly in favour of British independence, but it had always had a minority of members who rejected the established order. These rejectionists came to be the majority by the 1980s, by which time support for the ideal of liberal citizenship as 'membership' of the nation had been dwindling in favour of a culture of repudiation.[6] Today, there are still strong voices within the Labour movement who defend our national independence. Austin Mitchell MP has been steadfast in the Commons and Labour campaigners such as John Mills have been prominent in the wider Labour movement, but the majority of Labour MPs appear to embrace the EU with enthusiasm.

The atmosphere among many intellectuals, notably in the 20 years after the 'May Events' of 1968 in Paris, was increasingly hostile to liberal democracy. In May 1968, there had been huge student protests in Paris, and 11 million French workers (over 20 per cent of the population) had taken part in wildcat strikes and violent confrontations with the police. This sweeping hostility to 'the Establishment' spread to Britain and strengthened support for socialists influenced by Marxism who saw Britain as a nation run by a self-serving ruling class of wealthy people – the bourgeoisie. For these socialists, society and state were constructed to suit the interests of the ruling class, no more and no less. From the 1970s, class-war doctrines were supplemented by 'gender war'. It wasn't just the working class that was exploited by the ruling class but also women who were exploited by men. This movement was soon followed by race-based theories. Now it was minority ethnic groups who were oppressed by whites. Under the onslaught of multi-culturalism and post-modernism, the established order had few friends and defending Britain's heritage of freedom and democracy was seen by many in the Labour party as fighting for an illusion. This meant that, just as we faced an expansionist EU determined to weaken nation states and extend the power of Brussels, understanding of the merits of our own system was limited and opposition to 'the Establishment' was growing. The BBC played an especially discreditable role in promoting these ideas.

Movements supposedly against gender and racial discrimination and in favour of equality, in practice helped to undermine the social solidarity on which the free state relies. In particular they led to the growth of a predatory approach to law. Predatory litigation treated the law as a weapon for achieving financial gain or other material advantages. Instead of being a leveller, creating unity among diverse peoples, law became divisive. The tendency was heightened by attempts to impose law from the outside, usually seen as a kind of 'higher' law. Modern 'human rights' are claims by individuals at the expense of the wider community. They are non-territorial and, therefore, not connected with the give-and-take implied by living together under agreed rules. A free state is a community of law makers who seek the common good and submit to the same restraints. Law is the inherited outcome of living together amidst disagreement, not the orders issued by the ruler, or the impositions of a faction advancing its own interests. It is often said that rights imply duties, but together they also imply loyalty to a shared national system. Rights cannot be separated from duties and the call to duty relies on a common loyalty, rooted in reciprocity. By contrast, human rights are now often claimed by people who are simply taking advantage, as some notorious cases have shown.[7] When law becomes a weapon in partisan conflict, it can encourage antagonism and injustice. The upshot is that law making has been degraded into a weapon of sectarian struggle, when legislating should be about healing and pacifying divisions, not securing victory for any one faction.[8]

The case for resisting EU domination rests on a commitment to our longstanding ideal of a law-governed democracy, but if that ideal is no longer understood or shared it cannot be the basis of the allegiance that makes the nation state viable. This breakdown of our own solidarity allowed the EU to pursue a policy of 'divide and rule'. Sectarian groups in each nation state have been encouraged to look to Brussels to impose their views on other citizens. During the 1980s the Brussels elite aggressively sought to expand central powers at the expense of member states, but they needed individual nations to agree to hand over their powers and used whatever arguments worked in particular cases. In the 1980s the Labour party was persuaded to see the EU as a way of defeating Thatcherism. Jacques Delors cleverly exploited the frustration of the trade unions with Mrs Thatcher's policies. Previously suspicious of the EU as a 'capitalist club', the TUC came to see Brussels as an ally in imposing workplace regulations that would not be accepted by a Tory majority in Parliament. Moreover, some sectarian groups used Brussels to impose laws that were nominally anti-discrimination regulations, when in truth they were laws granting preferential treatment to politically-defined groups. Delors made no secret of his intention to supersede the nation state. In their excellent discussion of the emergence of the EU, David Craig and Matthew Elliott quote Jacques Delors in 1988. He predicted that within ten years '80 per cent of our economic legislation, perhaps even fiscal and social as well' would come from the EU and not from nation states.[9]

One of the most pernicious developments was the reversal of the burden of proof in workplace discrimination cases. Innocence until proven guilty has always been one of the bedrock principles of our justice system, until the EU got its hands on it. The Treaty of Rome (1957) provided for equal pay for men and women, and outlawed discrimination on grounds of nationality between citizens of member states. A directive on equal treatment for men and women was passed in 1976, but it was not until 1997, when the Treaty of Amsterdam amended the Treaty of Rome, that anti-discrimination was included as a basic founding principle of the Union.

Article 13 of the Amsterdam Treaty provides the European Union with a legal basis for the first time to take action to combat discrimination on grounds of race or ethnic origin, religion or belief, disability, age or sexual orientation. To give effect to Article 13, in 1999 the Commission produced two draft directives: the Employment Directive[10] and the Race Directive.[11] The Employment Directive required member states to make discrimination unlawful on grounds of race or ethnic origin, religion or belief, disability, age or sexual orientation in employment and training. The Race Directive required member states to make discrimination on grounds of ethnic origin unlawful in employment, training and the provision of services such as welfare and education. Member states were required to comply with the directives and had two years following adoption to introduce or amend their laws and procedures to meet the standards. Member states were also expected to ensure that their laws and administrative provisions, as well as employment contracts and collective agreements, were non-discriminatory.

In June 2000 the British Government accepted the Race Directive, even though it reversed the burden of proof. Essentially, any disproportionate impact on an ethnic group was *prima facie* evidence of discrimination and employers had to prove their innocence. The definition of 'indirect discrimination' in the Race Directive was any action that had a disproportionate impact on an ethnic group. Thus, if 10 per cent of the UK population belonged to an ethnic group, then 10 per cent of every sub-division of the population – including managing directors, the prison population, or university professors – should also be from ethnic minorities. If not, there was a presumption of discrimination.

Furthermore, the definition of discrimination was changed to make convictions easier to obtain. The 1976 Race Relations Act said that indirect discrimination occurred if a 'requirement or condition' was applied equally to persons of different racial groups but 'which is such that the proportion of persons from one racial group' who can comply with it is 'considerably smaller than the proportion of persons not of that racial group who can comply with it'.

The EU wording is less demanding requiring only that an apparently neutral provision or practice 'would put persons of a racial or ethnic origin at a particular disadvantage compared with other persons'. According to one of our most prominent experts in employment law, Sir Bob Hepple QC, in *Equality: a New Framework*, the EU Burden of Proof Directive[12] 'overcomes the need, under current UK law' to show that a 'requirement or condition' had a disparate impact. In other words, the EU Directive makes it easier to get convictions. The EU Directive, he says, also 'clarifies the test of proportionality' by setting out a test of 'substantially higher proportion'.

Hepple explains the difference between UK and EU law. At the time, the relevant UK law was set out by Lord Justice Neill in two main cases (*King v Great Britain China Centre* and *Zafar v Glasgow City Council*). Hepple writes that under UK law, if the employer fails to give a satisfactory reason for a difference in outcome, 'the tribunal *may* draw an inference' of guilt. Under EU law, says Hepple, the 'burden of proof shifts to the respondent to prove that there has been no unlawful treatment'. Hepple thoroughly approves, and recommendation 47 of his report said: 'There should be a statutory reversal of the burden of proof'.

Time and again in our history sectional groups, especially the wealthy, have tried to turn the law to their own advantage. Nevertheless our system of impartial justice has prevailed, despite occasional reverses. Consider the treatment of two groups in England in the eighteenth century: slaves and political activists. How were they treated in an age when the universal democratic franchise was only a dream? During the eighteenth century some wealthy people brought back slaves from the colonies. Sometimes they escaped and newspapers at the time contained adverts offering rewards for their recapture. And yet slavery had never been recognised in England. Matters came to a head in 1772.

James Somerset was an enslaved African who had been brought to England from America by his owner in 1769.[13] In 1771 he escaped and was recaptured. As a punishment, his owner put him on a ship bound for Jamaica, where he was to be sold as a plantation slave. Three English citizens, who claimed to be his godparents, applied to the Court of King's Bench for a writ of habeas corpus. The case was eventually heard by the Chief Justice of the King's Bench, Lord Mansfield. He ruled that the laws of England did not recognise slavery and that Mr Somerset must be released:

> ... the exercise of the power of a master over his slave must be supported by the Laws of particular Countries; but no foreigner can in England claim such a right over a man; such a claim is not known to the laws of England ... the power claimed never was in use here or acknowledged by the Law ... no Master ever was allowed here to take a Slave by force to be sold abroad because he had deserted from his service or for any other Reason whatever, we cannot say the Cause set forth by this Return is allowed or approved of by the Laws of this Kingdom; therefore the Man must be discharged.[14]

Wealthy people who wanted to keep slaves had attempted to turn the law to their own advantage. Lord Mansfield was a wealthy aristocrat who may well have sympathised with the slave owners but he did his duty according to law.

About twenty years later, after the French Revolution, the government was concerned about the activities of revolutionaries in the London Corresponding Society. Thomas Hardy, the Secretary of the society, was charged with high treason, but in 1794 an English jury acquitted him. The previous year, similar prosecutions had been brought in Scotland and harsh sentences of 14 years imprisonment had been imposed. In Scotland juries were not as independent as in England and were often manipulated by the authorities.

The Somerset and Hardy cases demonstrate the importance of upholding the law as the impartial protector of all, including the weakest members of society, such as slaves, or individuals who are disliked because of their political campaigning. Any weakening of impartiality, however slight it may seem when first introduced, can easily lead to the unravelling of our most fundamental protections. Laws that claim to be 'anti-discrimination', when they in fact grant preferential status to defined groups, breach this fundamental principle. Without the calculating desire of the EU elite to secure support by appealing to sectarian groups, these elemental breaks with our constitutional heritage would not have happened.

Immigration has also weakened national solidarity. A nation is based on allegiance and trust. Newcomers are by definition an unknown quantity. Where do their loyalties lie? Do they know anything of our island story? Are they hostile? Do they plan to make their homes here, or do they plan to work for two or three years while sending money to relatives overseas? Do they plan to work until they have saved enough to go back to their home country and buy their own home? If so, they may contribute a bit to our economic output in the short run but lack the long-term commitment to the future on which freedom depends. They are not going to make sacrifices today for the good of future generations.[15] The Brussels bureaucracy approves of such developments, not least because anything that weakens national solidarity tends to enhance their power.

Conservative divisions

During the 1980s, Brussels managed to convince free-market Tories that an extension of EU powers would help to reduce regulation, especially barriers to trade. As we have seen, it also simultaneously convinced the trade unions and the Labour party that Brussels would increase workplace regulation, by pushing through workplace laws that the Thatcher regime did not want.

From the late 1970s onwards, the Conservative party fell under the sway of free-market economists who defined the size and power of the state as the main political problem. Their solution was to reduce the scope of government. The smaller it was the better for everyone. Of course, recent British governments have undertaken many tasks which arguably would be better discharged within civil society, but an automatic presumption that less state action always equals more freedom cannot be justified. As we now know, a free society requires active government and every reduction in the powers of the state is not necessarily a gain for personal freedom. It is now infamous that so-called 'light-touch regulation' of financial services permitted an economic crisis in 2008 on a par with the Great Depression of the 1930s. The absence of government is what earlier philosophers had called the state of nature. From Locke onwards they had understood that freedom was only attainable in a civil society under which the state was, not the enemy of freedom, but its guarantor. Freedom is a political achievement, not a return to a harmonious natural state, where there is no coercion.

The free-market economists who dominated thinking throughout the 1980s and 1990s were resistant to the virtues of the 'free state', but they were keen on state action to remove barriers to trade and protect 'property rights'. And so when the opportunity arose in the mid-1980s to eliminate 'non-tariff barriers' and open the way for British companies to operate in Europe, they were glad to surrender British self-government in return for promises that the single market would be 'completed'. This amounted to putting the interests of large companies above those of the British people. These Tories defined freedom as 'less government' and, so long as the rhetoric of the Common Market was about free movement of people, goods, services and capital, they were happy. The Coalition continues to be drawn to the idea of 'completing the single market' and sees the EU as a way of forcing other European countries to make it easier for British companies to break into their markets. Completion of the single market has been promised since 1986 but never achieved because it was largely a ploy to garner the votes of free marketeers for extending EU powers. Tim Congdon was one of the first economists to see through it and has called it a trap.[16] Mrs Thatcher voiced doubts during her landmark Bruges speech of 1988: 'We have not successfully rolled back the frontiers of the state in Britain, only to see them re-imposed at a European level with a European super-state exercising a new dominance from Brussels.'[17] But in practice she opened the way to the imposition of greater 'harmonisation', as she herself conceded soon after she had left office.[18]

So long as significant groups in Britain regard Brussels as a friendly ally in forcing through measures without proper debate in Parliament, we are likely to witness continued erosion of self-government. A free state only works if we search together for the common good; not seeking to triumph over our opponents, but finding a reasonable way of living alongside one another. At first sight it seems paradoxical that our main political parties have not taken a clear stand in defence of our freedom, but Peter Oborne has skilfully shown how our main political parties became progressively divorced from their members. Leaders no longer see themselves as reflecting the opinion of the rank and file, or of the common good. They want power for themselves and view public opinion as something to be manipulated to achieve their objective.[19]

The realities of 'pooling' sovereignty

For several decades our independence as a free people has been defended under the banner of 'sovereignty'. EU enthusiasts typically advocate 'pooling' sovereignty instead of keeping it for ourselves. The implication is that the EU involves sharing (a good thing) and British sovereignty involves rejection of sharing, perhaps even selfishness. The choice is between working with other nations and refusing to work with them.

But this language wrongly describes what is at stake. There is a difference between voluntarily entering into agreements with other countries from time to time as the need arises, and permanently transferring power to make unknown future decisions to an outside agency that can't be controlled or removed if it makes a mistake. There are no doubt many beneficial agreements we will gladly enter into, as we have always done. But we do not want to be forced into agreements against our will.

The essence of a free society is mutual co-operation. The aim of liberal institutions is to facilitate a free life among people who disagree with each other, perhaps strongly. A liberal system is often said to be based on 'pluralism' and contrasted with a 'mass society', in which there is only the state and the individual. In a pluralist democracy it is usual to distinguish between three elements: the state; individuals; and people organised in powerful non-government institutions – civil society. These units of civil society need to be powerful enough to resist the abuse of state power, but not so powerful they could abuse their own powers. But such talk is completely alien to the leaders of the EU. The European Union exists to impose its own will. It has a civil-society programme, but it is an instrument for extending the power of the Commission. Funds are channelled to non-government organisations in many countries to enlist their political support and cut across national solidarity.

Moreover, the Commission's attitude to public debate is that once issues are settled they are a permanent part of the *acquis* of permanently settled laws and regulations. Our tradition is that no parliament can bind its successor. Discussion is never closed. By contrast, consider the attitude of the Commission to the discussion during 2013 about large-scale immigration and welfare benefits.

Viviane Reding, vice-president of the EU executive and Justice Commissioner, told Reuters: 'If Britain wants to leave the single market, you should say so. But if Britain wants to stay a part of the single market, free movement applies. You cannot have your cake and eat it, Mr Cameron!' On another occasion she said: 'Freedom of movement is non-negotiable as long as you are a member of the EU and the single market.'[20] In a true democracy an unelected official would not have the power to declare something 'non-negotiable'. Everything is up for per-petual discussion.

Laszlo Andor, the European Commissioner for Employment and Social Affairs, also attacked the British Government. He said that Mr Cameron's proposals were 'an unfortunate over-reaction'. EU rules, he said, applied equally to all 28 member states and had been accepted by the UK. He told the BBC *Today* programme that the British public had 'not been told all the truth' and that there were existing EU safeguards to prevent 'benefit tourism': 'We would need a more accurate presentation of the reality, not under pressure, not under hysteria, as sometimes happens in the UK. I would insist on presenting the truth, not false assumptions.' The prime minister's suggestions risked 'presenting the UK as a kind of nasty country in the European Union'.[21]

Presumably he thought his attitude was 'nice', but in truth he revealed a callous disregard for the harmful consequences on the host population of a sudden influx of newcomers. For him, EU doctrine must stand without regard to the effects.

European Commission President José Manuel Barroso also chipped in. He said he had spoken to Mr Cameron to remind him that free movement was a 'fundamental' EU principle 'that must be upheld'.[22] In an interview for the *Daily Telegraph*, he insisted that revision of the treaties was impossible:

> There are two ways. One is the pragmatic reasonable approach, seeing case by case whether legislation is needed or not. ... The other one is to have a fundamental discussion about the competences of the EU, even in terms of renationalisation. I think the second approach is doomed to failure. ... Britain wants to again consider the option of opting out. Fine, let's discuss it but to put into question the whole *acquis* of Europe is not very reasonable... What is difficult, or even impossible, is if we go for the exercise of repatriation of competences because that means revising the treaties and revision means unanimity. From my experience of 10 years, I don't believe it will work.

He expressed strong hostility to the repatriation of powers of self-government: 'I am for a stronger EU not a weaker EU,' he said. 'It is important we do this exercise in a pragmatic way avoiding what I call theological discussions about competences. Our approach is not an ideological one. It is not about weakening the EU. It is not about giving up on integration or on ever closer union.'[23]

Under our system, if a member of the executive spoke this way, Parliament would be rightly entitled to have them removed. Mr Andor's accusation that the UK Government's policy on immigration was 'nasty' and driven by xenophobia was typical of the venom often deployed by EU leaders.[24] Peter Oborne and Frances Weaver have painstakingly documented examples of personal attacks made during the campaign for the euro. Personal vilification was the stock-in-trade of euro supporters, with the BBC playing a particularly dishonourable role.[25]

Please may we have 'a more significant' role?

The aggressive expansionism of the Commission has gone so far that even diehard enthusiasts for the EU have spoken out. In a speech in December 2013, the UK's Attorney General Dominic Grieve found himself calling for national parliaments to be given 'a bigger and more significant role in the EU'. The proposal for a European Public Prosecutor, he thought, most strongly illustrated 'the extent to which some in the present Commission now seem dangerously out of touch with the people of Europe they are supposed to serve'.

This is how low we have sunk. Our Cabinet ministers are reduced to pleading with the Commission to allow national parliaments a 'more significant' role. Grieve accused the Commission of failing to observe the rule of law. Indeed it appeared to consider itself above the law:

Where is the practice of 'mutual sincere cooperation' promised in Article 4 of the Treaty on European Union? The Commission is a repeat offender here … in frequently demonstrating disregard for the prerogatives of the Council based on its own interpretation of its role under Article 17 TEU. I was frankly astonished to hear that the Commission

79

has recently signed a Memorandum of Understanding [MoU] with Switzerland in the absence of proper Council authorisation. Indeed, it appears that the MoU was signed at a time when the council was considering whether to grant such authorisation. I have to say that I find this case very troubling both as a lawyer and as a government minister.

He continued:

The Council is composed of government ministers answerable to electorates through their parliaments. By-passing the Council in this way not only breaches the inter-institutional balance, but also undermines the legitimacy of EU action. This would be bad enough if it were an isolated incident. However, it is not. This case is one of many.[26]

4

Internationalism and the EU

Even if the EU can be criticised for over-centralisation of power and an excessive desire to impose uniformity, should we not give it credit for bringing nations together and reducing the chances of conflict? Two main approaches to international relations are on offer today: the first envisages a world government enforcing the law everywhere under its control; while the other is based on mutual respect for legitimate differences.

Defence of any one nation state is sometimes attacked as a kind of xenophobia, presumably because it is assumed to imply hostility to other nations. However, as Roger Scruton has explained, we can usefully distinguish between two attitudes to other countries. Cosmopolitanism implies a person who feels at home in several different national cultures. Such individuals may not give their whole allegiance to one nation, but they are respectful of the others. It can be contrasted with internationalism, which implies hostility to all nations and aims for a single world power to impose its will. Far from being an admirable ideal, the desire for a single ruling power endangers us all.

Some enthusiasts for the EU quote Immanuel Kant as an ally, believing him to be a supporter of a policy of superseding outdated nations by a system of world government. They are familiar with Kant's view that there was no way of counteracting the will of rulers to subjugate others except a 'state of international right, based on enforceable public laws to which each state must submit (by analogy with a state of civil or political right ong individual men)'. He went on to say that upholding peace through a European balance of power was 'pure illusion'. And he continues with a line that goes down very well in Brussels: 'I likewise rely ... upon the very nature of things to force men to do what they do not willingly choose.'[1]

However, in his famous essay on 'Perpetual Peace', written a couple of years later in 1795, he strongly opposed a single international state and advocated instead cooperation between independent self-governing nations. He did so because he saw that a single world government would lack checks and balances. It provided no answer to the perennial political question: who guards the guards themselves? Under Britain's system, the power of the electorate to scrutinise and replace the government at election time 'guards the guards'.

Kant advocated a loose federation, which was 'to be preferred to an amalgamation of the separate nations under a single power which has overruled the rest and created a universal monarchy'. Under a centralised system, 'the laws progressively lose their impact as the government increases its range, and a soulless despotism, after crushing the germs of goodness, will finally lapse into anarchy'.[2]

He went on to advocate the creation of a 'kind of league' or 'pacific federation': 'This federation does not aim to acquire any power like that of a state, but merely to preserve and secure the *freedom* of each state in itself, along with that of the other confederated states.'[3] To avoid any doubt about his meaning, he said: 'a federation of this sort would not be the same thing as an international state. For the idea of an international state is contradictory, since every state involves a relationship between a superior (the legislator) and an inferior (the people obeying the laws)'. He goes on:

> a number of nations forming one state would constitute a single nation. And this contradicts our initial assumption, as we are here considering the right of nations in relation to one another in so far as they are a group of separate states which are not to be welded together as a unit.[4]

The states that made up the federation should be republics, not despotic states. By a republic he explains that he meant a state founded on three principles: the personal freedom of all members of society; the application of the law to everyone, without exception; and legal equality for all.[5]

To sum up: the aim of an international rule of law derives from an analogy between individuals within a state and countries within an international structure. Within a nation, internal security is provided by the rule of law and, in like manner, it is argued that war could be avoided by an international rule of law. But as Kant emphasised, everything human is unavoidably imperfect and so we should not aim for an 'international state' but only a loose confederation. As we have seen, Kant was scathing in one essay about the doctrine of a balance of power in Europe, but in later essays he advocated a federation, which implied several powerful states able to resist the others – a balance of powers. It is often forgotten that the rule of law within nations depends on checks and balances. Liberal civilisation depends on pluralism, which means in practice the presence of powerful private organisation able to hold the government to account, not least a free press.

Kant saw clearly that we must be on our guard against the abuse of power. Legislative, executive, and judicial power is always inevitably exercised by people who may abuse it for self-serving reasons. And unavoidable human fallibility also means that wielders of power are very likely to make mistakes. Thus, societies dedicated to freedom require that laws must be based on consent and that there must be an open process for changing them.

I have argued that we should defend the free nation state because it is the best safeguard for personal freedom. The EU elite tries to portray any defence of national self-government as narrow and self-serving, a sort of provincialism. And yet the EU itself is a project for the creation of a regional super-state – continental provincialism. It is not concerned about systems of cooperation between the governments of all free peoples. The Brussels bureaucracy appears to renounce all nationalism but on closer examination their alternative is not the universalism sought by internationalists, it is another kind of nationalism. A vast effort has been put, not into denouncing nationalism as such, but into building a rival nationalism, including a flag, symbols of EU citizenship, and an attempt to re-write history through its own EU museum.

Within the EU there have been some elements of inter-government cooperation, but they have been reluctantly accepted, not enthusiastically embraced. The true intentions of the elite that dominates the EU were declared by President Barroso in his 2012 'state of the union' address. He made it clear that the aim was to build a power bloc to rival the US and China. And he clearly envisaged an EU capable of exerting military force.[6] The world, he said, needs a Europe that is capable of 'deploying military missions'. Why? In part to 'stabilize the situation in crisis areas' but also to 'shape the world into a fairer, rules based and human rights abiding place'.

We should not be taken in by EU rhetoric. A far higher ideal than EU regionalism is to work towards the kind of international cooperation that respects the freedom of individual states and their peoples and seeks new ways of working together for the mutual benefit of all.

5

Conclusions

A state dedicated to upholding liberty is a political achievement not a natural condition that emerges when the state is minimised. We have achieved a shared allegiance to a way of living for which people will fight and die if necessary. They will fight for the sake of future citizens, not yet born. Even today, political leaders sometimes say that it would be wrong to impose a debt burden on our children, implying loyalty stretching across the generations. We have a life together, which is sometimes reflected in the political system and sometimes in voluntary action for the benefit of others. And we have friendly relations with numerous other countries, based on mutual respect.

The EU is bad for democracy, bad for personal freedom, bad for pluralistic civil society, and bad for international peace and cooperation.

It is bad for democracy because it is a power grab that seeks to take control away from nations that have been, and remain, the best safeguard against the abuse of political power. Such abuse remains one of the great problems faced by any state. Historically nations tended to be run by elites intent on expropriating wealth and power. Many countries still are. Democratic accountability under a liberal constitution has successfully contained the abuse of power in Britain and many other countries. A vital ingredient of constitutional democracy is national allegiance, a sentiment towards which the EU elite is unremittingly hostile. The only legitimate basis for the use of force by a government is that there has been consent, but Brussels decision makers are insulated from accountability. By contrast, our system from the earliest times allowed Parliament to exercise control over the income and expenditure of the executive and the policies of office holders. Even in the days of absolutism, policies were supposed to be based on 'counsel and consent'.[1] Chapter 2 described the unique features of the British constitution we have put at risk. Above all, the House of Commons can hold the government to account by calling an election at any time merely by passing a vote of no confidence. The power does not need to be used very often to have its effect. Its existence makes governments think twice before forcing through measures that the majority of people are against. But since we have joined the EU our own government does not pass all the laws that are enforced, and consequently our ability to remove the government without violence is of less importance.

Our strategy for accountability has been developed over many years. We can single out several vital components, all of which have been weakened by the EU. In addition to making our government removable by non-violent methods, we have as far as possible a government of laws rather than the personal commands of officials. And when discretion can't be avoided, we have made the heads of the executive conduct themselves in the open. We expect the government to state its aims so that they can be tested by experience and freely debated. Moreover, policies must be on a scale that renders them open to criticism and examination. We are not hostile to government as such but to unaccountable government and wary of utopianism when it is used as a disguise for unchecked power.

The EU is bad for personal freedom and for civil society because it opposes the free state, an approach to government that provides its people with a protected realm in which each can develop their beneficial capabilities to the full. In the free societies of the West people have opted to use their time and energy to foster personal responsibility and to advance civilisation by developing private associations for the public good. The EU compresses the realm of pluralistic freedom in its never-ending pursuit of harmonisation.

These claims are not unfamiliar, but it is perhaps surprising to hear a claim that the EU is also bad for international cooperation. Nor is it respectful of the freedom of other nations, especially that of its member states, which it is inclined to dismiss with a sneer as 'populism'. The EU is a new form of imperialism.

As Chapter 4 argued, the best basis for international cooperation is independent democracies that come together in a spirit of mutual respect for the independence of other nations. Nationality is not national self-seeking, but the only viable basis for peace between nations. Why? Because it provides checks and balances to overcome the abuse of power. The EU gains some credit from enthusiasts for international cooperation because it brings some nations together. But it is not true internationalism. Rather it is an attempt to construct a regional power bloc. The EU pretends to be against all nationalism, but is only against territorial sentiment that it regards as a rival to its own power. The EU also gets credit for opposing the aggressive nationalism that we associate with Germany and two devastating world wars, but the EU does not renounce all territorial loyalty. It promotes its own version of 'national' sentiment – European citizenship – by means of flags, anthems, a costly museum of European history, and more. It pretends to have achieved peace, but after World War Two Germany was incapable of fighting a war because it was disarmed and occupied. Above all, the EU is an aspiring regional power bloc defining itself against others, whereas the national loyalty of a free state is focused on creating the institutions that bring out the best in its own people and prevent the abuse of power. It wants good relations with similar states and avoids the creation of international structures whose power can be abused.

The Brussels bureaucracy typically tries to break down national allegiances. In particular it appeals to political elites in member states by offering money, perks and the trappings of office as well as the prospect of being able to impose their opinions on others. It tries to centralise resources so that Brussels can buy off organisations or industry sectors in member states. Groups such as farmers in France are amply rewarded, and 'structural' funds are channelled to many regions. The majority of the 28 nations are net recipients, which makes them more likely to use their votes in the Council to support the permanent bureaucracy.

The national stories of EU member states are very different, and we do not have enough in common for power to be exerted by whoever is currently in control in Brussels. There is no European demos, no shared culture, no confidence that groups will not seek to take advantage, no sense of the common good, no shared story of how we got to where we are today, no common view of obligations to future generations, no shared approach to law, and no common attitude to personal freedom, individual responsibility, civil society and the pursuit of public purposes in organised private life. Economic disparities remain large.

Nevertheless, it is important to keep reminding ourselves that, when we make a patriotic defence of our own independence, we stand up not only for our own interests but also the highest achievements of European civilisation. Europe's cultural and political heritage is ambiguous. In earlier times it spawned royal absolutism and more recently it has given birth to both modern fascism and modern liberal democracy. Two main tensions are relevant to the EU debate. First, there has been a longstanding dispute between, on the one hand, authoritarian rulers who want unfettered power to dictate policies and, on the other, supporters of government that is subject to constitutional limits designed to facilitate democratic accountability. Second, there has been a tension between groups that sought forcibly to impose one prescribed way of living and their rivals who preferred personal freedom. Britain has long been among the nations that attached the utmost importance to accountable government and possession of the personal freedom to choose the right way to live. Of course, choosing the best way to live implies the freedom to endorse traditional moralities that urge personal restraint. Many people throughout Europe share our commitment to civic and personal freedom and to constitutional democracy, and we should join them in a united struggle to build a consensus against what can only be called the new imperialism of Brussels.

Among the European countries that have a history of valuing their independence is Poland. She fought long and hard for independence against neighbouring countries that sought to dominate or partition her. Many other Eastern European countries remember Soviet domination only too well. The Netherlands recalls her battles against Spanish domination in the sixteenth century, while the Scandinavian countries have had more recent independence struggles. Norway was ruled by

Sweden until its independence in 1905. Iceland gained independence from Denmark in 1918 and Greenland was granted home rule by Denmark in 1979, leading to still greater autonomy more recently. We should urge the countries that share our love of liberty to join us in a confederation of nations that respects the freedom of other peoples and renounces Brussels imperialism.

Some say that the political culture on the Continent is radically different from our own, but there have been strong liberal currents of thought in the German-speaking world. In the nineteenth century von Humboldt was greatly admired by Mill, and in more recent times one the great champions of Western liberalism has been Austrian-born, German-speaking, Friedrich Hayek. He worked in America and England for much of his life but finished his career at the University of Freiburg. He is not an isolated case. He belonged to the tradition of Austrian and neo-Austrian economists whose influence has been international. After the Second World War the 'Ordo' liberals were important in determining the direction Germany took after the defeat of Hitler. They included Wilhelm Ropke and Ludwig Erhard.

In a wilfully devious attempt to take advantage of our sense of fair play, the 'club' analogy is often used to defend the EU and promote acquiescence in its numerous power grabs. If you join a club, the Brussels bureaucrat will say with a smirk, you must take the rough with the smooth. But the EU is not a club whose members joined in full awareness of what the rules were. The rules have been changed, without consent; not only without consent, but contrary to the known and declared wishes of the British government and people. A club that changes the rules, coerces members, and ignores their expressed views, is not a club in the ordinary sense we use the term.

It is an authoritarian structure that uses whatever after-the-fact rationalisations work in upholding its own dominance. A club entails 'give and take' and implies a common purpose.

We should restore our independence from EU control, not only to preserve our own heritage of constitutional democracy and personal freedom, but also because independent nations are the best safeguard for international peace and cooperation. The independent nation state, governed by a liberal-democratic constitution, discourages the abuse of power; and it confines the state to the protection of personal freedom, which entails freedom of association, which promotes pluralism, which in its turn further counteracts the concentration of power.

A Unilateral Declaration of Independence

This short book has focused on describing what is at stake, and a discussion of how exactly we can extricate ourselves is for a future project, but a hint of the direction of travel is merited. How can we regain our powers of self-government? Should we wait patiently for the referendum promised for 2017? Should we re-negotiate in the hope that something good might come of the process? Or should we take more rapid action?

First we need to rebuild our own sense of national loyalty, which means not seeking sectarian laws and not going above the head of parliament to the EU or the Strasbourg court. The two traditional 'sides of industry' have been most at fault in looking to Europe to impose their views. As Chapter 3 showed, the TUC thinks of Brussels as an ally in defying the preferences of the British people expressed through the Parliament of the day. Some business lobbies have also used the Brussels machine to get their way, most notoriously when, in the vain hope of 'completing' the single market, they urged the surrender of the UK's veto over numerous vital areas of policy. Unless we can put a search for the common good at the heart of our political process, little will be gained from any EU strategy.

Above all, we need to restore parliamentary sovereignty, which means we should restore the authority of the majority of the British people acting through Parliament. We should make explicit the primacy of Parliament by amending the 1972 European Communities Act and declaring our own Supreme Court to be a higher authority than any other court. Henceforward, laws passed by Parliament would be superior to any EU laws. This would amount to a unilateral declaration of independence, but would not imply immediate renegotiation of every law and regulation. We could take our time and go through the numerous unwanted laws one by one. In any event, many regulations governing trade are unavoidable. When we export to any nation, inside the EU or not, it is necessary to accept their regulations. But in such cases the regulations do not need to affect how we govern companies that produce only for the home market.

Some of us will be reluctant to 'break' the law, and it is precisely our loyalty to law that is now being exploited by the EU. But the fact is that many nations have already flouted EU laws, most notably Germany and France when they ignored the budget and debt requirements agreed when the euro was established. Because of their importance to the EU project, nothing was done. We should follow their example and challenge the EU to do its worst.

As Chapter 2 showed, Lord Denning concluded in 1979 that an explicit resolution of Parliament declaring the supremacy of UK law would bind the British courts. In a pamphlet for the Bruges Group written in 1990, he said that Parliament 'can repeal or amend the 1972 Act so as to make the decisions of the European Court of Justice not binding unless approved by our own House of Lords [now the Supreme Court]; and to make the directives not binding unless approved by the Secretary of State'.

Lord Justice Laws reiterated the supremacy of Parliament in the case of Thoburn v Sunderland City Council in 2003 (the 'Metric Martyrs' case):

> Parliament cannot bind its successors by stipulating against repeal, wholly or partly, of the ECA [European Communities Act]. It cannot stipulate as to the manner and form of any subsequent legislation... Thus there is nothing in the ECA which allows the Court of Justice, or any other institutions of the EU, to touch or qualify the conditions of Parliament's legislative supremacy in the United Kingdom. Not because the legislature chose not to allow it; because by our law it could not allow it. That being so, the legislative and judicial institutions of the EU cannot intrude upon those conditions. The British Parliament has not the authority to authorise any such thing. Being sovereign, it cannot abandon its sovereignty... This is, of course, the traditional doctrine of sovereignty. If it is to be modified, it certainly cannot be done by the incorporation of external texts. The conditions of Parliament's legislative supremacy in the United Kingdom necessarily remain in the United Kingdom's hands.[2]

While delivering a Hamlyn lecture in 2013 he quoted his earlier remark and affirmed his commitment to his earlier opinion.[3]

Lord Judge, the Lord Chief Justice from 2008 to 2013, has also recently emphasised the importance of the doctrine of parliamentary sovereignty. He said in a lecture delivered in 2013:

> The consequence of the sovereignty of Parliament is that whether they like it or not, judges are bound to apply an Act of Parliament even where that Act provides for the application of judicial authority from a foreign court. This was the result of the European Communities Act 1972. The position of the judiciary is frequently misunderstood. Judges have no choice. They are bound by British law to follow the rulings of the Court of Justice of the European Union in Luxemburg. Our judiciary cannot set aside the law enacted by Parliament, nor suspend it nor dispense with it. To do so would contravene the Bill of Rights. Exactly the same principle applies to the enactment of the Human Rights Act 1998. The courts are required by domestic legislation to implement the European Convention of Human Rights just because the Human Rights Act is legislation enacted by Parliament.

Much of his speech was devoted to the human rights court in Strasbourg, but the essential principles apply to the European Union's Luxembourg Court. Lord Judge said that: 'To take account of the decisions of the European Court does not mean that you are required to apply or follow them. If that was the statutory intention, that would be the language used in the statute.'

He proposed that Parliament should make a declaration of the legal position:

> It would, I believe, make sense for s2(1) of the 1998 Act to be amended, to express (a) that the obligation to take account of the decisions of the Strasbourg Court did not mean that our Supreme Court was required to follow or apply those decisions, and (b) that in this jurisdiction the Supreme Court is, at the very least, a court of equal standing with the Strasbourg Court.

He expressed his preference for parliamentary sovereignty unequivocally:

> My personal belief is that parliamentary sovereignty on these issues should not be exported, and we should beware of the danger of even an indirect importation of the slightest obligation on Parliament to comply with the orders and directions of any court, let alone a foreign court.[4]

A similar approach could easily be taken to the jurisdiction of the Luxembourg Court, which enforces EU law. Parliament should stipulate that, if any law enacted by Parliament contradicts EU law, including case law, then Britain's courts are bound to enforce the law as it was enacted by Parliament and to take no account of EU law.

The EU has usurped our power to uphold liberal civilisation. We must take back our independence, even if there is some inconvenience in the short run. It will be worth it.

Endnotes

1 Simons, H., *Economic Policy For a Free Society*, London: University of Chicago Press, 1948.

2 Hayek, F., *The Road to Serfdom*, London: Routledge, 1944, pp. 13-14.

3 Mill, J.S., *Considerations On Representative Government*, New York: Prometheus, 1991.

4 Quoted in Moore, C., *The EU vs the Nation State: Who's Winning?* London: CPS, 2012, p. 22.

5 Rotherham, L., *The EU in a Nutshell*, London: Harriman House, 2012, pp. 323-29.

6 Quoted in Miller, D., *On Nationality*, Oxford: Clarendon Press, 1997, p. 5.

7 Wells, H.G., *The Outline of History*, London: Cassell, 1951, p. 1192.

8 Scruton, R., *England and the Need For Nations*, London: Civitas, 2006; Minogue, K., *The Servile Mind*, London: Encounter, 2012; Moore, C., *The EU vs the Nation State*, London: CPS, 2012; Miller, D., *On Nationality*, Oxford: Clarendon Press, 1995; Goodhart, D., *The British Dream*, London: Atlantic, 2013.

9 Collier, P., *Exodus: Immigration and Multiculturalism in the 21st Century*, London: Allen Lane, 2013.

10 If true, this is a great relief, given the calibre of some our current leaders.

11 Dibelius, W., *England: Its Character and Genius*, London: Harper, 1930, p. 504.

12 Dibelius, p. 504.

13 Miller, *On Nationality*, pp. 23, 185.

14 Miller, *On Nationality*, p. 27.

15 Fukuyama, F., *The Origins of Political Order*, London: Profile, 2011.

16 Green, D.G., *Individualists Who Co-operate*, London: Civitas, 2009.

17 Locke, J., *Two Treatises of Government*, (edited by Peter Laslett) Cambridge: Cambridge University Press, 1988, pp. 284, 306, 363.

18 Acton, J., *The History of Freedom and Other Essays*, London: Macmillan, 1907, p. 52.

19 Milton, J., *Areopagitica*, Indianapolis: Liberty Fund, 1999, p. 45.

20 Minogue, *The Servile Mind*, pp. 4, 6, 8, 214.

21 Locke, J., 'The Second Treatise of Government' in Locke, J., *Two Treaties of Government*, London: Cambridge University Press, 1988.

22 Kant, I., *Political Writings*, (edited by Hans Reiss) London: Cambridge University Press, 1991, p. 46.

23 'Letter to a Member of the National Assembly', 1791, in *The Works of the Right Honourable Edmund Burke*, Boston: Little Brown, 1866, vol. 4, pp. 51-52.

24 Minogue, *The Servile Mind*, p. 159.

25 Macaulay, T.B., *History of England*, 4 vols, London: Heron Books, 1967 edn., vol. 1, pp. 229-30.

26 Acton, J., *The History of Freedom and Other Essays*, 1907, p. 52.

27 Federalist Papers.

28 Minogue, *The Servile Mind*, pp. 178, 146.

29 Locke, J., *Some Thoughts Concerning Education*, Cambridge: Hackett, 1996.

30 Minogue, *The Servile Mind*, p. 160.

31 Minogue, *The Servile Mind*, pp. 167-68, 173.

32 Minogue, *The Servile Mind*, pp. 173-74

33 Ruggiero, *The History of European Liberalism*, London: Beacon 1959, p. 354.

34 Frankl, V., *Man's Search For Meaning*, London: Beacon, 1946.

35 Dennis, N., *Rising Crime and the Dismembered Family*, London: Civitas: 1993, chapter 4.

36 Minogue, *The Servile Mind*, p. 74.

37 Minogue, *The Servile Mind*, p. 220-21.

38 Owen, D., *English Philanthropy 1660 – 1960*, London: OUP, 1965.

39 Loch, C.S., *Charity and Social Life*, London: Macmillan, 1910, pp. 411-12.

40 Mayhew, H., *London Labour and the London Poor*, (A Selected Edition.) London: OUP, 2010, p. 389.

41 Green, D., *Reinventing Civil Society*, London: Civitas, 1993.

42 Beveridge, Lord, *Voluntary Action*, London: Allen & Unwin, 1948, p. 92, p. 328.

43 Thompson, E.P., *The Making of the English Working Class*, London, Gollancz, 1980, pp. 40-53.

44 For an excellent account see Schama, S., *Rough Crossings*, London: BBC, 2005.

45 Minogue, *The Servile Mind*, p. 172.

46 Collier, P., *The Bottom Billion*, Oxford: OUP, 2008.

47 Acemoglu, D. and Robinson, J.A., *Why Nations Fail*, London: Profile, 2012, pp. 7-9.

2: What Have We Lost?

1   Freeman, E.A., *The Growth of the English Constitution*, London: Macmillan, 1898, pp. 91, 100; Maitland, F.W., *The Constitutional History of England*, Cambridge: Cambridge University Press, 1908, p. 55.

2   Stubbs, W., *The Constitutional History of England in its Origin and Development* (three vols), Cambridge: Cambridge University Press, vol. 1, pp. 27, 41.

3   Maitland, *The Constitutional History of* England, London: Cambridge University Press, 1946, pp. 55-56, p. 58.

4   Stubbs, vol. 1, pp. 135-36; Maitland, p. 60.

5   Stubbs, vol. 1, pp. 267-68; Maitland, pp. 60-61.

6   Maitland, pp. 97-98.

7   Stubbs, vol. 1, p. 528; Maitland, pp. 64, 68.

8   Stubbs, vol. 2, pp. 90-93; Maitland, pp. 70-72.

9   Maitland, pp. 100-03.

10 Stubbs, vol. 3, p. 13; Maitland, pp. 190-92.

11 Stubbs, vol. 3, pp. 240-46; Maitland, pp. 198, 201.

12 Maitland, pp. 194-96.

13 Freeman, p. 106; Anson, W., *The Law and Custom of the Constitution*, Oxford: Clarendon Press, 1892, part 1, pp. 20-21; Maitland, p. 199.

14 Freeman, pp. 131, 134.

15 Freeman, p. 137, note pp. 217-18.

16 Maitland, p. 284. Freeman, note p. 217.

17 Freeman, p. 155.

18 Freeman, p. 144.

19 Freeman, p. 147, note p. 220; Freeman, 153; note p. 230.

20 Maitland, p. 300.

21 Coke, E., 'Reports' in Sheppard, S. (ed.), *Selected Writing of Sir Edward Coke*, Indianapolis: Liberty Fund, 2003, p. 264.

22 Coke, p. 275.

23 Coke, p. 195.

24 Coke, p. 195.

25 Coke, p. 224.

26 Coke, p. 225.

27 Maitland, pp. 304, 301.

28 Maitland, pp. 253-54, 257-58.

29 Maitland, pp. 263, 303, 305-06.

30 Maitland, pp. 261, 307, 298, 308.

31 Anson, part 1, p. 23; Maitland, pp. 310, 435.

32 Maitland, pp. 310, 313.

33 Anson, part 1, pp. 29-30; Maitland, pp. 388, 395.

34 Freeman, p. 120.

35 Freeman, p. 123; Maitland, pp. 395-96; Anson, pp. 29-30.

36 Maitland, p. 405.

37 Dicey, A.V., *Introduction to the Study of the Law of the Constitution* (1915 edn), Indianapolis: Liberty Fund, 1982.

38 Dicey, p. 285.

39 Dicey, pp. 285-87.

40 Dicey, p. 286.

41 Dicey, p. 287.

42 Dicey, pp. 287-88.

43 Dicey, p. 302.

44 Dicey, p. 288.

45 Freeman, pp. 115-17.

46 Dicey, pp. 290-91.

47 Schama, S., *A History of Britain*, London: BBC, 2009, vol. 2, p. 9.

48 Cannadine, D., *G.M. Trevelyan: A Life in History*, London: Penguin, 1992, p. 197.

49 Davies, N., *The Isles: A History*, London: Macmillan, 2000, p. 329.

50 Davies, *The Isles*, p. 698.

51 Butterfield, H., *The Whig Interpretation of History*, London: Norton, 1965, p. 12, p. 30.

52 Butterfield, p. 92.

53 Benda, J., *The Treason of the Intellectuals*, London: Transaction, 2007, p. 187.

54 Butterfield, p. 109.

55 Macaulay, T., *The History of England*, vol. 1, p. 2.

56 Macaulay, p. 378.

57 Macaulay, pp. 386-87.

58 Bradley, A.W. and Ewing, K.D., *Constitutional and Administrative Law* (14th edn), London: Pearson, 2004,

p. 141; Loveland, I., *Constitutional Law, Administrative Law, and Human Rights* (4ᵗʰ edn), Oxford: OUP, 2006, p. 445.

59 The Maastricht Treaty was signed in December 1991 and ratified in 1992.

60 Quoted in Craig and Elliott, *The Great European Rip-Off*, London: Random House, 2009, p. 83.

61 Felixstowe, [1976] 2 Ll L Rep 656.

62 *Macarthys Ltd v Smith*, [1979] ICR 785.

63 *Macarthys Ltd v Smith*, [1979] ICR 785, 789; Bradley and Ewing,
p. 144.

64 Wade, H.W.R., 'The basis of legal sovereignty', *Cambridge Law Journal*, vol. 13, no. 2 (Nov. 1955) pp. 172-97; Wade, H.W.R., 'Sovereignty—revolution or evolution?', *Law Quarterly Review*, 1996, 112 (Oct.), pp. 568-575.

65 R *v* Secretary of State for Transport ex parte Factortame Ltd (No. 2), [1991] AC 603. See also Loveland, I., 2006, pp. 480-82.

66 HC Deb., 15 Feb. 1972, col 274; Bradley and Ewing,
p. 142.

67 Bradley and Ewing, pp. 142-43.

68 Bradley and Ewing, p. 143.

3: Why Independence Matters

1 See:
http://ec.europa.eu/public_opinion/archives/eb/eb79/eb79_first_en.pdf

2 http://europa.eu/about-eu/institutions-bodies/council-eu/

3 Rodrik, D., *The Globalization Paradox*, Oxford: OUP, 2011.

4 Booker, C. and North, R., *The Great Deception: A Secret History of the European Union*, London: Continuum, 2003.

5 OPEC: The Organisation of Petroleum Exporting Countries.

6 Scruton, R., *England and the Need For Nations*, London: Civitas, 2006; Scruton, R., *The West and the Rest*, London: Continuum, 2002; Minogue, *Servile Mind*, p. 67.

7 Abu Qatada, for example, had been convicted of terrorist crimes in Jordan but used human-rights laws to resist deportation for years, until 2013.

8 Minogue, K., *The Servile Mind*, London: Encounter, 2012, p. 387.

9 Craig, D., Elliott, M., *The Great European Rip-Off*, London: Random House, 2009, p. 81.

10 http://eur-lex.europa.eu/LexUriServ/LexUriServ.do?uri=CELEX:32000L0078:en:HTML

11 http://eur-lex.europa.eu/LexUriServ/LexUriServ.do?uri=CELEX:32000L0043:en:HTML

12 http://eur-lex.europa.eu/smartapi/cgi/sga_doc?smartapi!celexplus!prod!DocNumber&lg=en&type_doc=Directive&an_doc=1997&nu_doc=80

13 Sometimes spelt Sommerset, or Somersett.

14 Schama, S., *Rough Crossings*, London: BBC, 2005, p. 60.

15 Collier, P., *Exodus: Immigration and Multiculturalism in the 21st Century*, London: Allen Lane, 2013.

16 Congdon, T., *How Much Does the European Union Cost Britain?*, UKIP: 2012.

17 http://www.margaretthatcher.org/document/107332

18 Thatcher, M., *Statecraft*, London: Harper Collins, 2002, p. 372.

19 Oborne, P., *The Triumph of the Political Class*, London: Simon & Schuster, 2008; *Daily Telegraph*, 2 January 2014.

20 http://www.euractiv.com/video/reding-freedom-movement-non-nego-532002

    http://www.reuters.com/article/2013/11/27/us-britain-immigration-ec-idUSBRE9AQ0WZ20131127

21 http://www.bbc.co.uk/news/uk-politics-25114890

22 http://www.bbc.co.uk/news/uk-politics-25114890

23 See:
    http://www.telegraph.co.uk/news/worldnews/europe/eu/10350956/Jose-Manuel-Barroso-David-Camerons-plan-to-claw-back-powers-from-the-EU-is-doomed-to-failure.html

24 http://www.bbc.co.uk/programmes/p01mk9f1

25 Oborne, P. and Weaver, F., *Guilty Men*, London: CPS, 2011.

26 Grieve, Dominic, Speech in Brussels, 2 December 2013, 'The future of Europe: opportunities and challenges'.

4: Internationalism and the EU

1 Kant, I., 'On the common saying: This may be true in theory, but it does not apply in practice' in Reiss, H. (ed.) *Kant: Political Writings*, London: Cambridge University Press, 1991, p. 92.

2 Kant, I., 'Perpetual Peace: A philosophical sketch' in Reiss, H. (ed.) *Kant: Political Writings*, London: Cambridge University Press, 1991, p. 113.

3 'Perpetual Peace', p. 104.

4 'Perpetual Peace', p. 102.

5 'Perpetual Peace', p. 99.

6 President Barroso, State of the Union address, 2012.

5: Conclusions

1 Green, D.G., *What Have We Done? The Surrender of Our Democracy to the EU,* London: Civitas, 2013.

2 Laws, L.J. in Thoburn [2003] QB 151, para 59.

3 Lord Justice Laws, 'Lecture III: The Common Law and Europe', Hamlyn Lectures 2013, 27 November 2013.

4 Lord Judge, Constitutional Change: Unfinished Business, Lecture, 2013.